"A great question that all achievers ask themselves, and one which Simon helps us to explore with an in-depth look at the conversations that go on in the minds of some of life's inspiring achievers, who all answered that question … and did it!

If you are asking yourself that question, this book is a vital tool in your toolbox; it's a powerful team mate.

Buy it. Read it. Do IT!"

Andy McMenemy, world class endurance athlete and award winning inspirational speaker

"A refreshingly honest read and thankfully completely devoid of hype. Loaded with practical advice on how to achieve your potential that will both inspire and engage you."

Paul McGee, The SUMO Guy, international bestselling author and speaker

"The mindsets, approaches and techniques in *Could I do that?* are exactly what helped me to win two Olympic Gold medals, and Simon has a great way of bringing these to life so anyone can take these principles and apply them to their world."

Steve Williams, OBE, double Olympic gold medallist

"The average lifespan is 4000 weeks. And the chances are, yours are whizzing by in a blur! Read Simon's book and do something BIG!"

Andy Cope, bestselling author of *The Art of Being Brilliant* and happiness expert

"If you've ever had a dream which seems out of reach, or a challenge that seems too big or too daunting, this book is for you. Find out how to achieve what you thought was impossible."

Claire O'Hara, kayak and squirt bo...

COULD I DO THAT?

SIMON HARTLEY

CAPSTONE
A Wiley Brand

This edition first published in 2014
© 2014 Simon Hartley

Registered office
John Wiley and Sons Ltd, The Atrium, Southern Gate, Chichester, West Sussex, PO19 8SQ, United Kingdom

For details of our global editorial offices, for customer services and for information about how to apply for permission to reuse the copyright material in this book please see our website at www.wiley.com.

Library of Congress Cataloging-in-Publication Data

Hartley, Simon.
    Could I do that? / Simon Hartley.
        pages cm
    Includes bibliographical references.
    ISBN 978-0-857-08480-4 (pbk.)
    1. Motivation (Psychology)   2. Ability—Psychological aspects.   3. Success—Psychological aspects.   I. Title.
    BF503.H375 2014
    153.8'3—dc23   2013047981

A catalogue record for this book is available from the British Library.

ISBN 978-0-857-08480-4 (paperback) ISBN 978-0-857-08477-4 (ebk)
ISBN 978-0-857-08478-1 (ebk)

Cover design by Mackerel Ltd   Internal pages designed by Andy Prior Design Ltd

Set in 10/15pt Frutiger Lt Std by Toppan Best-set Premedia Limited, Hong Kong
Printed in Great Britain by TJ International Ltd, Padstow, Cornwall, UK

Contents

Foreword

Gripping the reeds, I crawled out of the freezing water up to my neck on a pitch black night in the middle of Dartmoor. I'd fallen into a hidden crevasse during a night navigation exercise with the Ice Warrior team, training with for what will be my toughest challenge yet; an 800 mile, three month expedition to the centre of the Arctic. The expedition has thwarted many explorers and our destination remains a place which has never been reached by any human beings. If successful, we will not only enter the history books, but we will be able provide a greater scientific and environmental understanding of the impact we have on the planet.

I have not entered into this challenge frivolously; it is perhaps an understatement to say that it will be immeasurably dangerous. There are countless unknowns, not to mention the cost. We are hoping we will be able to mitigate some of these with acute preparation, planning and risk analysis. As this book will remind you, if you fail to plan, then plan to fail.

It wasn't always like this. By the time I left school, I'd been bullied, failed every exam and been arrested as part of a shop lifting gang of nine boys. I was a good kid, but I was easily impressionable and my self-esteem was non-existent. But, I guess there must have been an adventurous streak in me; I'd also completed two tall ships races, spent five years training as a high board diver and completed the Gold Duke of Edinburgh award as a sea cadet. These were my passions, being active and outside. At 13, I had a few jobs; including paper rounds and door-to-door lottery cards. It seems that being an entrepreneur was also in my nature.

I've noticed that life is never straightforward. Challenges are inevitable; it's how we deal with them that is important.

After my 17th birthday, I joined the Royal Navy. I signed a 22 year contract and I loved it, but that wasn't to be. After nearly 10 years, I was medically discharged with a severe respiratory problem, within a year I was a civilian. I was devastated, I felt institutionalized and very lost.

My answer was to use this experience as an opportunity to change my life. I made the decision to start running and set out to run the London marathon, which I did in less than four hours. I also needed to work so I became a highboard diving coach. But the money was poor, so I started my first business; a sports shop. To be honest, I didn't have a clue about running a business and fewer than 18 months later, the business folded and all of my savings were lost. So, whilst working in factories, I began studying business and accountancy and completed a software and IT engineering diploma. I started again for the third time. Within a few years I was thriving as an IT consultant in the Dot.Com Boom in London and what a ride that was!

My recovery was short lived and in February 2002 it all ended. Whilst out on my bike, training for the London Triathlon, I was hit head on by a car and broke my back. Life became very difficult and extremely painful. I was no longer active and this had a serious impact on my mental and emotional wellbeing. I was not just physically broke, but again financially.

Often the challenges we're presented with can appear daunting, sometimes seemingly impossible. It's tempting to wonder whether we can do it. We may contemplate whether we have the energy or the strength to overcome what we have been presented with.

Experience has proved to me that it is our mind and how we listen to it and act, which determines whether we succeed or fail. Without realizing it, I found myself using the approaches that you'll find in this book to overcome my own challenges throughout my life.

My recovery took nearly six years. I got back on my feet and ran the Chicago marathon in 2008. Since then I've run, swum and cycled over 6,500 miles. I've climbed the highest mountain in Russia in freezing temperatures of -30 degrees. I've completed ultra runs, long distance swims and an Ironman.

But life loves to continue to throw us challenges and change is inevitable. In 2012, all within 4 months of each other, I lost the business I'd spent a decade building, my long term, toxic relationship ended and both grand-parents died from cancer. Financially, emotionally and intellectually, I had a break-down.

I've been forced to start again many times. I've picked myself up, and turned break-downs into break-throughs. I took personal responsibility for my life; I got active, developed my spirituality, examined my passions in life, made plans and took decisive action. Being physically active has helped to keep me going and I now focus on helping others through the organization I founded, Take a Challenge. With over half a million visitors to the website since its inception, Take a Challenge has helped to inspire others to change their lives through the inspirational stories of everyday people achieving extraordinary things. Now, through the principles contained within this book, you can too.

Christopher Brisley
Founder and CEO of Take a Challenge

www.takeachallenge.org
Anything is Possible

Twitter: @CBrisley

Introduction

Human beings are capable of some truly astonishing feats.

On 30th April 2008, David Blaine held his breath underwater for a world record breaking 17 minutes and 4.4 seconds, live on the Oprah Show. Wow!

In 2007, Lewis Pugh swam a kilometre in the Arctic Ocean at the North Pole. It took him 18 minutes and 50 seconds. Conventional wisdom tells us that hypothermia takes effect when our body temperature drops below 35 degrees Celsius. The water temperature at the North Pole for Lewis' swim was 1.7 degrees below zero! That's impossible, right?

If you think that sounds bizarre, John Evans balanced a car (yes, a real, live 159 kg Mini Cooper) on his head for 33 seconds; no hands. Amazingly, it's a Guinness world record, not an April Fool (Guinness World Records, 2012).

It's tempting to think of these things as "impossible", or that the people who have achieved these incredible feats are "superhuman". How long can you hold your breath? One minute? Two? Three? I think I'd be surprised if I managed 60 seconds. Are these people made of "different stuff"? Do they have magical powers? I guess that depends on your definition of "magic".

Illusionist, David Blaine (2010), said…

"I think magic, whether holding my breath or shuffling a deck of cards, is pretty simple; it's practice, it's training and it's experimenting while pushing through the pain to be the best I can be. That's what magic is to me".

"If he can do it, could I?"

Have you ever said the words, "I wonder if I could do something like that"?

Even if you haven't said them out loud, have you said them to yourself? Have they been a part of the conversation in your mind? When I look around me, I see more and more people attempting, and achieving, incredible things. Did you know that there were 127 new Guinness world records established in the London 2012 Olympic Games alone (Guinness World Records, 2013)? Of course, world records are not confined to athletic events. In 2009, Dean Gould broke the world record by flipping 71 beer mats whilst blindfolded. As I sit here typing this, there is a radio station in Doncaster, UK, that is attempting to break the world record for the longest ever show. At 4 pm this afternoon they will have been broadcasting for 80 hours non-stop. Whilst I have never had an urge to flip beer mats or be on the radio for 80 hours, I have definitely thought of taking on a real challenge. As I look on, I can't help asking myself if I could do something exceptional as well. What's stopping me?

Do you get that nagging feeling that you're not completely fulfilling your potential? Do you suspect that you have more to give? Would you also like to close that gap between what you've achieved so far and your true potential?

As a sport psychology consultant, I have always been interested in elite performance. I have been intrigued to know what differentiates exceptional performers from the rest. For several years I have been studying world class performers, to understand what sets them apart and what common characteristics bind them all. I've been rubbing shoulders with some incredible people, who have achieved some pretty extraordinary feats; such as climbing all of the world's 8000-metre mountains, completing unsupported polar expeditions, running back-to-back ultra-marathons and winning mammoth adventure races. I had the great pleasure of getting to know them as I wrote *How To Shine*; the book in which I share the eight common characteristics that I found.

In fact, writing *How To Shine* was a mission for me. For many years, I've been fascinated by world class performance. I've been on a quest to find out how world class performers think, what they've experienced, how they've approached their challenges and what makes them tick. However, it seems that somehow I've become infected by them as well. Time after time I have heard world-class performers describe themselves as "ordinary people". They all seem to have a very modest start point. They don't seem to have been imparted with any innate talent from birth.

Their achievements don't appear to be the result of luck or simply because they were in the right place at the right time either. If they can do it, surely we can too.

The Inspiration

As I wrote *How To Shine* I found myself typing the words, "Where is the limit?", "Where are the boundaries anyway?" and "Do you know where your limit is?" As I wrote the words, and read them back to myself, I felt an uneasy realization starting to dawn. I suspect that I am very similar to many people. I have no idea where my limits are. I don't know where the boundaries of my potential lie.

It struck me that most of us have no concept of where our limits are. We know where discomfort starts, sure. But do we know where our ceiling is? Do we have any idea of what we are capable of? Although I've pushed myself, I also know that I've spent my life working well within my potential. If I'm honest, I have no idea where my limit is! It is unexplored territory and it's time I started to understand it.

The same is true of most people; even those of us who are on a quest for perpetual self-improvement are unsure where their limitations are. Even if we feel that some things are beyond us, we often do so instinctively rather than through evidence. Do you know where your true limits are?

And so, I have set myself a challenge. Powered by the question, "Could I Do That?", I am going to embark upon a rather ridiculous endurance challenge. I'll explain exactly how ridiculous it is shortly.

However, this book is not really about my challenge. In fact, the challenge itself is largely irrelevant. It is about how to take on challenges. In particular, it is about how to tackle those challenges that seem huge ... daunting ... impossible.

> ## "I'd rather regret the things I've done than the things I haven't done."
>
> *Lucille Ball, American comedienne and actress*

Your Challenges

When you uttered those words, "I wonder if I could do that" (even if they were just to yourself), what challenge were you contemplating? Did you also say, almost in the same breath, "I'd love to do it, but there is no way I could" or "well, I wouldn't know where to start"?

Have you seen performers on stage, or on TV, or watched people running marathons, and thought, "I'd love to be able to do that"? Have you watched *Masterchef, Britain's Got Talent* or *Great British Bake Off* and thought "I'd love to do something like that"? Have you ever dreamed of turning your business idea into reality, or releasing your creative flair by writing the book that's been incubating in your mind or making a short film? Do you often hear the words, "I really ought to ...?" or "one day I'll ..." echoing through your mind?

If we're honest with ourselves, I'll bet we all have challenges that we would love to take on. But, for some reason, there is a gap between us and what we'd love to achieve. The question is ...

how can we bridge that gap? How do we overcome the "stuff" that currently stands between us and our potential?

In this book, I'd like to explore how our minds work when we engage in challenges. What actually goes on in those "little grey cells"? What does it think like and feel like? I'm going to learn about how to take on a significant challenge from the inside, and I'd like to share this first-hand experience with you as I go. We can learn those universal and transferable lessons, which can be applied to any challenge.

Do You Fancy a Journey?

Do you fancy a journey into a slightly warm, damp, dark and squishy place?

I'll bet you don't get invitations like that every day. Are you excited? Have I sold this to you yet?

The place I'm referring to is my brain. More specifically, I'd like to invite you into my mind and my thoughts. I'll walk you through the "challenges within the challenge" that I've experienced in my own endurance event, and help illustrate how they translate to any challenge – whether they are physical, mental, entrepreneurial or habitual. I know that my daft endurance event is going to throw up a host of challenges of its own. And yours will too – regardless of what your own challenge might actually be. Most of these "challenges within the challenge" will be mental wrestles. There is going to be a conversation going on between your ears; a battle for supremacy between your desires and your fears. There will be a tug of war between your dreams and your doubts, and probably a voice shouting "okay, stop now, I've had enough". Part of this mission, then, is to conquer this internal mental territory.

Along the way, we'll reflect on how the mental attributes required for such a challenge are developed. In *How To Shine*, I noticed the toughness that many world-class performers display. Andy McMenemy ran ultra-marathons with a torn Achilles tendon. Bruce Duncan injured his leg two hours into "The Epic Tri" and still pushed himself for the next six days to complete the challenge. Alan Hinkes was convinced that he was going to die at the top of a mountain, but mustered the strength to descend. And Michael E. Thornton ran into a gun battle, and got shot twice, in order to rescue his friend and teammate.

Through my studies of world-class performers, and my work with elite athletes, I've consistently found that they are all mentally tough. The problem is, I'm not. The truth is, I'm a bit of a wimp. I have an incredibly low pain threshold. I squeal when my wife plucks in-growing hairs or squeezes a spot on my back. When I'm training, I tend to slow down when I get short of breath or my muscles start to burn. Am I cut out for this? Am I a tough person? Are you? When was the last time you pushed yourself to the limit and managed to push through rather than stepping back when things became painful? There's no shame in doing that – it's normal.

It's tempting to think that if I'm not tough right now, I'll never be tough enough. However, like any attribute, toughness is developed. How do we build the mental armour? This journey is going to help us understand the attributes required to succeed AND how we develop them.

It's Not Just Me

As our journey unfolds, I'd like to draw on the wise words of a few friends of mine that have also taken on significant challenges, arguably much tougher challenges than mine. As well as my own mental wrestles, I'd like to share some of theirs. Understanding how they tackled their challenges can also help us to take on ours. They have been there, done it and have the merchandise to prove it. Their journeys highlight some of what lies ahead for us. Their experiences can help illustrate those valuable universal lessons and help us to navigate our own challenges.

I'd like to introduce you to…

★ Andy Reid

Andy was a corporal in The Yorkshire Regiment of the British Army who served in Helmand Province, Afghanistan. In October 2009, Andy was severely injured by an improvised explosive device (IED). Amazingly, he survived the injuries, but lost both of his legs, his right arm and a finger on his left hand. Andy's own challenge started the moment that IED exploded.

★ Steve Williams

Steve is a double Olympic champion. He has rowed alongside Sir Matthew Pinsent and James Cracknell, as part of the legendary Great Britain coxless four crew. He won two Olympic gold medals in Athens 2004 and Beijing 2008. Steve is also a four-time World Champion and received an OBE in 2009.

Aside from his extraordinary success as a rower, in 2011 Steve skied to the Geographic North Pole and summited Mount Everest in back-to-back expeditions.

★ Robyn Benincasa

Robyn is a world champion adventure racer and holder of Guinness world records for extreme endurance challenges. She's competed in over 40 multi-day, multi-sport adventure races; she has also set world records in 24-hour kayaking. Robyn is also a San Diego firefighter and heads up a charity called Project Athena.

★ My brother, Jon Hartley

Jon is a regular bloke who made the bold decision to move from the UK and set up both a new home and a brand new business in Germany. When he made this decision he didn't speak more than a few words of German! Now that's some challenge.

All of these people have pearls of wisdom and valuable insights that we can use in our own quest.

Finding Your Challenge

How do you decide upon a challenge? How do you go from knowing that you want to do something, to having an idea that is fully formed, clearly defined, with a magnetic quality that makes it irresistibly engaging?

I started out knowing I wanted to do something that really challenged me. However, to begin with I didn't know what. As I let my mind get to grips with the question, a number of ideas began to surface. I spent a while working through them and imagining them. One idea led to another and before long, I had a few possibilities. I'd been inspired by the ultra-endurance athletes, so all of these ideas were based on daft physical endurance events. If I hadn't already started a number of businesses and flexed my entrepreneurial muscles, I may have looked at this as the challenge for me. Equally, if I hadn't published my first book, I could well have seen authorship in the same way. I've already started to take on these challenges and begun to test myself in these domains. However, I know that I've not really pushed my physical boundaries, so this really captured my imagination.

I played around with a number of possibilities. It's almost like trying on different clothes to see what fits best or which ones suit the occasion. Should I try to extend somebody else's achievement by going further or doing more? What about adapting challenges that I'd read about or heard about? At one point I had three or four contenders. All of them were tough challenges. However, as demanding as they were, there was one idea that set off those sparks of excitement and got the adrenaline running. There was one challenge that I kept coming back to and kept imagining. Whenever I thought about it, a smile would cross my face. It excited me and intrigued me. I began daydreaming about what it would be like and working out how I might attempt it. In my experience, that's when you know you've got it.

So, what is it? What's my ridiculous challenge?

Could I kayak from London to John O'Groats (north eastern most tip of Scotland) … and then cycle from John O'Groats to Land's End (south western most tip of England) … and then run from Land's End back to London? It's a journey of more than 2000 miles. It includes almost 900 miles kayaking in the North Sea, around 900 miles on a bike and over 300 miles of running. Could I do all this in under 40 days? Now that would be an epic challenge! It also appears that it's a challenge that nobody has attempted before. Individual elements have been done, but it seems that no one has combined them into one challenge.

Interestingly, when other people start off on extraordinary challenges, they often have similar start points. Their ideas gradually surface, grow and take hold.

Robyn Benincasa explained that she'd read about expedition racing in a magazine and it just appealed to her. She knew that she was at her best in the longer races, where things got uglier. She was fascinated by the prospect of racing in a team and how she could match up against the terrain.

My brother, Jon, had discussed the idea of moving to Germany with his partner Astrid over a long period of time. They had got to a point where they'd made the decision to move without really realizing it. It was just a question of knowing when the "right time" was. For Jon, this was the end of the football season, because he was working in football, and for Astrid, it was finishing her university studies. Naturally then, this helped them to identify the right time to make the move.

Who has inspired you? What do you aspire to achieve? What ideas do you have, however crazy they might seem? What are those ideas that you find yourself daydreaming about? Are there thoughts that seem to be accompanied by the words, "I wonder if I could ...?" or "It would be amazing if I could ..." or "I couldn't possibly ... could I?" When you unleash your imagination, where does it go? If you take those tethers off and abandon "common sense", what do you imagine? What are the adventures that you dream of? If you weren't inhibited by all those self-limiting words of caution, what would you do? In the words of a friend of mine, "If you knew you couldn't fail, what would you try?"

Is there something that, when you imagine it, causes you to smile and sets off those sparks of excitement?

Chapter 1

The Inception

"First comes thought; then organization of that thought, into ideas and plans; then transformation of those plans into reality. The beginning, as you will observe, is in your imagination."

Napoleon Hill

W hat happens in your mind when you think about the idea for your challenge? Do you hear a voice saying … "That's a ridiculous idea. Surely I couldn't do anything like that, could I?"

It's tempting to dismiss thoughts like this before they take hold. I guess it is similar to seeds that fall on the ground but never germinate or take root. Whilst they are still embryonic, these ideas are at their most vulnerable. It would be so easy to crush them with a thought such as, "That's just bonkers, there's no way I could do that" or, "I wouldn't even know where to begin" or, in my case, "I'm not an endurance athlete".

How often do we use our own self-perception to limit our potential? Do we subscribe to the notion that if we haven't done it before, we're not capable of doing it? I wonder how many people throughout the course of history have conceived of great inventions but never developed them, simply because they don't see themselves as "an inventor". How many great businesses have never existed because the person with the idea "wasn't a business person"? How many times have you been frustrated by a product that doesn't quite do what you need, and said the words, "Someone ought to invent a …"? How many times have you heard friends say, "Why doesn't someone come up with a …"?

WE ALL HAVE OPPORTUNITIES TO BECOME EXCEPTIONAL

I suspect that it is in these moments that many billionaires are born. In these tiny, split-second moments in time, we all have opportunities to become exceptional. Sparks are being ignited all the time inside our minds. Each one is an idea that could potentially change your life, and potentially the lives of other people too. Some people take these sparks of inspiration and nurture them. They actively seek out ways to explore the ideas further, to fuel them and grow them. Others let them die out. Perhaps it is this characteristic that differentiates entrepreneurs. Maybe it is their willingness to invest in the ideas, these tiny sparks, and give them life.

Sparks are being ignited all the
time inside our minds.

In the movie, *Inception*, Dom Cobb (played by Leonardo DiCaprio) describes how an idea is like a virus:

"Resilient, highly contagious. Once an idea has taken hold of the brain it's almost impossible to eradicate. An idea that is fully formed, fully understood, that sticks, right in there somewhere" [he points to his temple].

"… And even the smallest seed of an idea can grow. It can grow to define or destroy you … "

So how do we ensure that our ideas survive and grow? How do we start to bridge that gap between us and what we'd love to do? How do we begin to take that spark and start to create flames?

I suspect that the answer is embarrassingly simple. Imagine, for a moment, that you simply didn't kill the idea at the point of inception. What if you didn't dismiss it immediately? What would happen if you entertained it for a while, pondered it, mulled it over and even began to imagine embarking upon it? Thankfully, we can do this all within the safety and privacy of our own minds. We don't have to tell anyone else about it straight away. We don't have to risk humiliating ourselves. We don't have to try it and fail. In the safe confines of our mind, we can let it incubate. The truth is, we can begin to give our idea life just by resisting the temptation to snuff it out.

Of course, not all ideas are good ideas. As Dom Cobb said in *Inception*, these ideas have the potential to define or destroy. Some ideas are probably best squashed. However, it is the other ideas, the good ones, which we need to give our attention to. These good ideas might look a little scary, but perhaps that's not a great reason to dismiss them.

**Good ideas might look a little scary, but perhaps
that's not a great reason to dismiss them.**

From Ground Zero

It is very easy to think of all the reasons not to do something. There are always potential hurdles and barriers. Tough challenges are never easy (the clue is in the word "tough"). As we know, they're also the most fulfilling. It's entirely possible that you'll be bombarded with a myriad of thoughts as you conceive of your challenge. If your life is already full to bursting point with day-to-day tasks, responsibilities and duties, how on earth are you going to fit in another major challenge? If clearing your inbox seems daunting enough, where do you find the time and energy to really push yourself? Sometimes, in just managing what we have in front of us, we can feel like we're already pushing ourselves to the limit. However, it's not quite the same as doing something that truly extends us. Managing the demands of our day-to-day life is not the same as embarking upon a potentially life-changing adventure. And, whilst it may be satisfying to clear down our inbox, exploring our potential can be deeply enriching. It's always possible to find the reasons not to engage with those challenges that seem to take on almost epic proportions. Sometimes we need to balance this by also understanding the reasons to engage.

There are an awful lot of very good reasons for me not to take on this ridiculous challenge. Did I mention that I'm not an athlete?

My starting point is the same as many other people. As this challenge was born in my mind, I was running three to four miles a couple of times a week. Very few of my runs exceeded half an hour in duration. My weekly mileage didn't normally reach double figures. In fact, before I started training for this event my longest ever run was a half marathon, which I ran three years previously. And my greatest sporting achievements? Well, I played under-18s football for Yeovil Town (don't snigger) and represented my university in rugby league. It's not spectacular is it?

I didn't own a road bike and hadn't been on a bike for over six months when I started this. My longest ride ever was 19 miles, which I did when I was a 12-year-old boy scout. In my adult life, the longest cycle ride was around 12 miles, so I think it's fair to say that I'm a novice on the bike too.

I haven't got any real adventure experience. I haven't climbed any mountains, kayaked around the UK or swum across any oceans. I once hiked up Ben Macdui (the second highest peak in Scotland) with some friends when I was at university, around 15 years ago, but that's as close as I have come. I don't have any equipment or massive resources. I can't just buy what I need, or take huge amounts of time off to train, plan and prepare. I have a life, a family and work, just like most other people. I run my own business so there is a constant need to balance time in the business and time with the family.

With a young family, cash is tight, so I can't just solve problems by writing cheques either.

I think it would be fair to say that I'm starting from scratch. From my perspective, this makes any challenge much tougher. It's not simply a case of honing skills that I already have, because I don't have any. I don't have the option of drawing on my experiences either, because I don't have any. In fact, I don't have many reference points at all for this challenge. In some ways, this naivety is probably an advantage. There are no reference points, so there are few self-imposed limitations. A cyclist might consider that 200 miles a day sounds ridiculous, if their own personal best is around 100 miles. A marathon runner might say the same about running consecutive ultra-marathons. However, with no reference points, there are fewer limitations. The mind is free to work on the basis that the targets are all possible. All I have to do is work out how to achieve them.

> "In 2004, at the age of 26, I set out to cross the Arctic Ocean from Russia to Canada. At the time there were panels of experts saying that it couldn't be done. Fortunately, no one told me."
>
> Ben Saunders, polar explorer, who I interviewed when I wrote How To Shine

Sometimes it helps not to know what everyone else perceives to be possible. If we don't know that a challenge is "impossible", we're free to carry on as if anything is possible.

Interestingly, double Olympic gold medallist, Steve Williams, was not a natural athlete when he was young. He explained that his school, at the time, was a modest rowing school with modest ambitions. Added to that, he was a late developer. Steve remembers being either last or second to last in the school cross country and struggling to make the second team in sports. Like many kids, he had dreams of becoming an Olympian but it took a long time before his dreams translated into a genuine ambition.

If Steve can go from being last in the school cross country to becoming a double Olympic champion, maybe there's hope for me! Ben and Steve show that it doesn't matter if you have absolutely no direct previous experience. You don't need to be "a natural" either. Everyone has to start out somewhere, even the best in the world. You can set out without a track record in the challenge you want to take on, you just have to work out how to do it. Many of us might conclude that coming last in the school cross country must mean that we're just not athletic. Surely if you're no good at sport at school, the idea that you could become Olympic champion is simply ridiculous. Steve Williams shows that your past does not equal your future!

What If Your Challenges Choose You?

What if you don't choose your challenge? What if it chooses you? Andy Reid didn't choose to have both of his legs and his right arm blown off by a Taliban IED. He explained that his challenge started as he awoke in Selly Oak Hospital in Birmingham, after being flown back from Helmand Province in Afghanistan.

"When I woke up I was in the UK; it was two days after the IED exploded. The doctor explained what had happened and that I'd lost my arm and my legs. To be honest, I wasn't that surprised when he told me because I knew there was nothing where my arm and legs had been. I just thought, 'well, I'm still here and there are friends of mine who aren't'. I thought to myself, 'I'm a survivor not a victim'."

Andy went on to explain that the first stage was to accept what had happened.

"I knew I'd lost my legs, I'd accepted it. I joined the Army, I knew the risks and so I took responsibility for what happened to me. So I began thinking, 'Okay, what's next? What do I have to do?'"

For many people, Andy included, the challenge can seem daunting, almost overwhelming. However, having accepted it, he decided to take it on.

Sometimes our challenges do choose us. I've been made redundant twice so far in my life. Both occasions presented me with a challenge. In these situations there is an opportunity to engage with the challenges and take them on. Of course, we also have the choice to back away from them and to disengage. Denial can masquerade as the comfortable option at times. Andy Reid could have chosen that path too. He could have opted to become a victim and settle for life in a wheelchair. Perhaps our perception of these opportunities dictates how we approach them. Do we see them as a challenge or as a threat? Do we focus on the potential to come out of the experience stronger, or the chance of failure? In many ways we're presented with these opportunities – some big, some very small – every single day. Some people recognize them, others don't. Some people embrace them, others decline. What do you tend to do?

To help an idea take hold and grow we need to invest in it.

From Inception to Commitment

Wherever it comes from, in order to help an idea take hold and grow, we need to invest in it and cultivate it. We need to spend time thinking about it and allow our imagination to play with it. If we do this, we could even start to feel excited about the prospect.

Ultra-marathon runner, Andy McMenemy, describes how he feels "a tickle of adrenaline" when he starts to conceive of a new challenge. This simple process helps us develop an emotional connection to our ideas. If a challenge is exciting, it is more likely to engage us.

Have you heard of S.M.A.R.T.E.R. goal setting? Each letter relates to a word that apparently helps us to set goals effectively. You'll find that there are several versions, but here's a fairly common one: Specific, Measurable, Attainable, Realistic, Time-bound, Evaluate, Relevant.

I wonder if Walt Disney followed SMARTER principles when he conceived of the idea to build Disney World. He decided to take a swamp, several miles outside of Orlando, and invested millions of dollars building a giant fairy-tale princess castle on it. Imagine the conversations that he must have had when he positioned the idea with his bank manager. Does his idea appear SMART? How many people would have described it as "attainable", "realistic" or "relevant"?

I suspect that my goal setting process for this challenge would be more accurately described as D.U.M.B.E.R. That stands for Daft, Unrealistic, Mental, Bonkers, Exciting, Ridiculous.

Which one sounds more engaging to you? Which one is more likely to ignite your passion?

Personally, I'd advocate DUMBER goals.

In order to commit to something fully, we need to be able to immerse ourselves in it. To do that, we need to love it. It's very similar to marriage (now marriage really is a challenge … oops, sorry love!). This is also true of our challenges. We need to be able to fall in love with them in order to dedicate ourselves to them completely. It is no surprise to me that the world class performers I've met all have a deep passion for what they do. Passion and love go hand in hand.

So, how do we develop a love and passion? Life experience tells us that we could experience that "love at first sight", or "lightning bolt" moment. Sometimes it might be as simple as being struck by Cupid's arrow.

However, sometimes falling in love happens more slowly. Often we'll start by liking something, then liking it quite a lot, then really liking it and eventually loving it.

My brother, Jon, explained his reason for giving up a comfortable job and life in London to start a business in Germany. It all started when he took trips to Germany for the World Cup, to watch football, to visit Oktoberfest, and so on. He began to appreciate German culture and German football. Over the course of several years he became enamoured with it all and started to imagine life in Germany; what life might be like and how to adapt to a new culture. Jon was also looking for a new challenge. He'd lived in the US but was intrigued by the challenge of living in a country where English is not the first language. He'd also reached a point in his profession where he was looking for the next challenge. It seems that the combination between yearning for a challenge and this intrinsic love sparked Jon's decision to make the move.

Just for a moment, put yourself in Jon's shoes. Imagine that you've started to envisage life in a foreign country and that you've become excited and curious about the prospect. Imagine also that to make this a reality you need to make a leap of faith; leaving your comfortable, familiar life and knowing that when you make that move you'll feel completely out of your depth. How would you feel? What would you do?

To allow our ideas to grow, we need to allow them to germinate, let the roots take hold and nurture them for a while. Your own mind is like a nursery; it gives them a safe space and an environment in which they can flourish. By resisting the urge to judge them, or squash them, we give them a chance to engage us and excite us. These ideas might look a little scary, but maybe that's not such a bad thing. And then there comes a time when we start to wonder what it would be like if this idea were to become reality; a time when we decide whether we are willing to commit ourselves to it. If we want to take our idea from inception to commitment, maybe we simply need to fall in love with it first. Those who become successful often have a complete devotion to what they do. In short, they really, really want it.

Chapter Summary

★ Do you have challenges you'd love to take on, but haven't dared to attempt?

★ How can you bridge the gap that stands between you and what you'd love to achieve?

★ What would happen if you resisted the temptation to squash your ideas?

★ What if you allowed yourself to entertain them for a while?

★ Are your current goals SMARTER or DUMBER?

★ Are you in love with your goals?

Chapter 2
The Why

"He who has a *why* to live, can bear almost any *how*."

Friedrich Nietzche

Viktor Frankl was a Jewish psychiatrist, living in Vienna at the outbreak of World War II. As you can imagine, Austria was not a great place to be at a time when Nazi Germany was gaining power in Europe. Because he was a respected academic, a number of US universities offered him the opportunity to escape Europe and take up residence in the United States. Frankl turned them down, choosing instead to stay with his family. Soon afterwards, he and his family were captured by the Nazis. They were separated and taken into concentration camps. Not long after being sent to Theresienstadt, Viktor Frankl learned that his father had died at the hands of the Nazis. During the next two years he also lost his mother and new bride. He endured years of suffering as he moved from camp to camp. In his book, *Man's Search for Meaning*, Frankl describes both the incredible adversity that he and the other prisoners experienced, and also how they coped. He noticed that those with a strong reason to live often survived. However, if their reason faded, they quickly followed.

As I was writing *How To Shine*, I listened to people describe the way they'd taken on epic challenges and found a common theme emerging. Record-breaking polar explorer, Ben Saunders, told me that when he and his team first start out on a new challenge, they have no idea how they will achieve it. When they're taking on a challenge that no one has ever done before, there is no blueprint. Although they may not know how, they do know why.

Steve Williams also understands that his reason to row was all-important, and extended beyond simply winning a medal. I've had many similar conversations with Olympians. On the face of it, they're motivated by the gold medal. But a medal is just a metal disc. What does winning a gold medal mean to them? Olympians dedicate years of their lives to this. They get up at 6.30 am, aching and sore, six or seven days a week, pushing themselves to the limit. What makes that metal disc worth the effort? Steve Williams explained that one of the best days of his life was taking his gold medal, from Athens, to his nephew's school in Australia to do a "show and tell". That's what made it all worthwhile.

Andy Reid explained that his motivation to walk again was powered by the desire to walk down the aisle to marry his fiancée (now wife) Claire. He also had visions of standing on the parade ground next to his fellow soldiers; not sitting in a wheelchair. These overwhelming desires helped Andy to navigate all of the hurdles and setbacks that he encountered. This mindset also applies to business. Many of the world's great business leaders describe their companies as "not only for profit". In his book, *Small Giants*, Bo Burlingham (2007) studied the motivation that drives a group of exceptional entrepreneurs who deliberately build businesses that are great, rather than big. In many cases their raison d'etre is to serve their community.

"I know that it's

1% inspiration

and

99%

perspiration,

but try doing this
without the 1%."

Many other people that have achieved incredible feats echo this sentiment. If we have the why, we are often able to find the how.

So, What's the "Why"?

For me, very simply, I want to answer the question "Could I Do That?" I want to know how far I can go; to explore my potential. It might seem like a strange answer. You may be thinking, "And ...? Surely there must be something else."

What's your reason for taking on the challenge you have chosen? What is it that's driving you to do this? What's your "why"?

I'm fascinated by motivation. At the heart of our motivation is our reason; our "why". However, our motivation often has several layers to it. There is often a range of different motives at play, not just one.

For example, there might also be a bit of me that wants others to notice, to respect me because of this challenge. Is this an ego booster? Am I doing this to look good? Is there a part of me that likes people saying, "Wow, that sounds amazing"? What about the fundraising? How much of my motivation for this challenge is driven by a desire to raise money for charity? What about professional status and profile? Is this challenge a way of raising my profile so that I can sell more books, secure more professional speaking engagements and grow my business? To be honest, there have to be easier ways to raise my profile than this!

The point is that we rarely have just one motivational driver. As with many things, these motives are not created equally. Some of them are absolutely central, whilst others are peripheral. Some really do matter, whilst others exist on a "take it or leave it" basis. Often we don't question them or test them; we just use them to fuel our motivational fire. However, there are times when they do get tested. It is important to know that sometimes, when tested, our motives can fail. Rather than waiting for circumstance to test them as we take on our challenges, we can actually assess whether our motives are central or peripheral.

The Acid Test

Have a think about some of the challenges that you're tackling at the moment. What is your "why", or perhaps I should ask, what are your "whys"? Like me, I'm sure you'll have lots of potential reasons to take on your challenge. Which ones are absolutely central, and which are not?

The acid test is to take away some of those reasons and find out what effect it has on your motivation. Sometimes, if we take away one of our reasons it will have little or no impact on our motivation; we'll continue on as if nothing had changed. However, there are some motives that are so central that we find it hard to continue in their absence. If I am motivated to start a business by a dream of having a big salary, a huge house and shiny new sports car, my motivation could falter if I am working all the hours God sends and I'm just about scraping by. There is a chance I could end up thinking, "What's the point in all this?" If my reason to start the business was to follow my passion through my profession, to be my own boss and to take pride in my work, it's less likely that my motivation will be dented as long as I'm making a living.

I'll use myself as a guinea pig to illustrate the point. Let's take those potential motives that I outlined a moment ago. What if I embark upon this challenge and fail? What if I don't look good? What if I look like a complete spanner? My track record suggests that it is quite likely. My first session in the kayak lasted less than 10 minutes, before I fell out. Far from carving gracefully and effortlessly through the water, my boat was upside down and I was swimming back to the shore, towing my paddle. I also fell off my bike on the first serious ride. My loving wife regularly tells me that I look like a complete idiot dressed up in my cycling gear. There are some people that look quite good in Lycra. I am not one of them. I'm just not a good shape for skin-tight clothes. If you add a couple of buckets of sweat and the inability to walk properly after sitting on a razor blade for several hours, you'll get the picture. I haven't mastered the art of walking in the cleated cycling shoes either. So, if I was in this to look good, my motivation would evaporate very quickly.

There are some "usual suspects", which tend to form our human motives. As you think about your desire to take on a challenge, start to reflect upon how strongly these might feature.

What about the respect from others? It is arguably one of the strongest motives that we have in the modern world. Why do people work so hard to get the big house, the big car with the fancy badge, the swanky new clothes or even the new job title? What's it all for? If we're completely honest with ourselves, the badge on the front of the car doesn't always relate to its comfort or reliability. Most people would admit to buying certain brands because of the "prestige" value that comes with them. The same is probably true of postcodes, labels in the back of clothes, or on shoes, or handbags. Is the pair of shoes with the designer label vastly different than the pair next to it at a tenth of the price? The fact that people buy fake designer goods tells us a lot. Sometimes the badge on its own is enough; we don't even need the quality that goes with it. If we took all the badges off, would we really know one from the other? So, what's it all about? Perhaps this is all driven by our desire to garner respect from those around us.

How about the desire to increase our profile, get noticed, increase income or step up the professional ladder? Do we do all of this because we want to be seen as "successful" in the eyes of our peers?

Using the "acid test" we can see the impact that these potential motives have. What if you successfully completed your challenge but no one noticed, your income was unaffected or it made no difference to your professional position? Would it still be worth it, or would it seem like a waste of time?

From my perspective, it would be lovely if some of these things happened as well, but their absence does not detract from my motivation. I'm intrigued by this challenge. I am curious to know just what I'm capable of. On one day last autumn I set myself a mini-challenge; to run a marathon in a day. It was a regular Tuesday in the office. I started with a ten mile run before breakfast, did another six after lunch and then ten before bed. It is not a run that I had to do for my training. I did it because I was curious. I wanted to know whether I could.

Understanding your "why" gives you a firm foundation as you take on your challenge. Arguably, our motivation is the one factor that has the single greatest impact on our success.

When we know our true reason, we also understand the circumstances that may trip us up. We can start to foresee potential issues before they arrive. And, we can become aware of just how strong and stable our motivation really is; what threats can our motivation survive, and which might sink us?

What Difference Does it Make?

I am a great believer that having a reason is not always enough. Having the right reason, I believe, is crucial. As we've seen, motivation can evaporate if your primary motive disappears. If I was doing this challenge for profile and I struggled to generate media coverage, I may end up thinking "What's the point in all this?" The same principle is true in a business context. Last year I delivered two Be World Class conferences. Although the two conferences last year were not the first, they were the first that we had delivered as a company. Previously we had joined forces with event management and media partners. We're not an event management specialist, so launching and delivering these conferences was a big challenge for us. It required a lot of hours and an enormous effort. When we set out we had some pretty ambitious expectations on the amount of income that we'd generate. A few months into the build-up we realized that we were a long way off the targets. At that point we had a decision to make. Do we continue, knowing that we might make very little return for our efforts, or stop? This decision is ultimately underpinned by our reason for launching the conferences in the first place. Was it solely to make money? No, that wasn't the only reason. We also wanted to host an event that would have tremendous value to the business leaders that were attending. We wanted people to leave the event inspired, and go on to tell others how valuable it was. In doing so, we hoped to build a solid platform for future events. We also wanted to allow more people to understand what we are about and develop an appetite for more. So, we kept going. The events just about broke even, which is not a great financial return for the hours of effort. However, in almost every other respect, the events were hugely successful.

There are many points along our journeys when we hit potholes, roadblocks and many other traffic-halting analogies. In these moments we are faced with decisions and choices. Do we go on or do we call it a day? These are the times when we rely upon the power of our "why". Have we got a reason that is capable of sustaining us? Is it stable and enduring? Is it robust enough to survive?

Let's imagine two people, called Alan and Bernard, who set out on a similar challenge: to climb a mountain. Alan is climbing this mountain because he just wants to climb ever higher and more challenging peaks. He's not really bothered whether anyone else notices, or admires him for it. Alan loves being out in the hills, loves taking on new climbs and pushing himself to new levels. Bernard, on the other hand, is a very ambitious bloke who likes to be successful in everything he does. You might say he's an "achievement junkie". He loves taking on challenges in both his business and personal life. He describes himself as a "winner" and achieves everything he sets out to do.

Alan and Bernard have decided that they'd both like to climb a little-known mountain called Everest (I believe it's somewhere in Asia). They're both aware that it is going to be pretty expensive, dangerous and will require a lot of time, training and preparation. Bernard is pretty wealthy and runs a successful business, so finds the time and money that he needs relatively easily. Alan, on the other hand, needs to raise the funds himself and fit in all of his training and preparation around other work.

In preparation for their Everest expedition, they need to do some training climbs. Alan enjoys them but Bernard sees them as a means to an end. He does them almost begrudgingly, and often gets frustrated along the way. He tends to become impatient quickly and annoyed if things don't go as planned. Alan is having a great time. Rather than getting upset if things go wrong, he just sees it as a bigger challenge, which makes the climb more interesting and demanding.

When they get to the base camp on Everest, the weather conditions deteriorate and they are forced to wait it out. Being stuck at base camp for any length of time is uncomfortable; living in a tent, in sub-zero conditions and eating dehydrated food. Alan doesn't view this as hardship. Bernard, on the other hand, grows tired of it very quickly and starts to get impatient. Many climbers abort the mission at this stage because they're not able to sit it out at base camp and wait for the conditions to improve. Instead they conclude that this is all "pointless", so they turn around and head home. One of the dangers in this situation is that climbers do the opposite. Their impatience leads them to attempt a summit of the peak too early. The result, often, is that they die in their attempt. The temptation to try for the summit is much greater, of course, if your reason for being there is based on achieving an outcome. Imagine that your reason to climb was to reach the summit. What would you do if you were less than 100 metres from the peak when the conditions turned against you? If you were driven by the need to reach the peak, you might decide to go on. If you were motivated to simply climb as high as you could, you'd probably be happy to go back and try again another day.

Bernard's reason for being there is likely to present him with a very uncomfortable decision: to attempt the climb in bad weather and risk death, or to turn around and admit defeat. For an "achievement junkie", that's a tough call. Alan's decision is pretty easy. He's much more likely to stay on the mountain and enjoy being there until the conditions allow him to climb safely.

What do you think happens next?

"Don't aim at success – the
more you aim at it and make
it a target, the more you're
going to miss it. For success, like
happiness, cannot be pursued;
it must ensue, and it only does
so as the unintended
side-effect of one's dedication
to a cause greater than oneself
or as a by-product of one's
surrender to a person other
than oneself. Happiness must
happen, and the same holds
for success: you have to let it
happen by not caring about it."

Viktor Frankl (2004)

Viktor Frankl, thank you for being!

What's More Important?

Have you ever noticed that your choices and decisions are often made according to your perception of importance?

Sometimes you decide to do something that you don't particularly like doing because "it's important". Essentially, you're saying that it is more important to put yourself out and do it than to sit back and leave it undone. Many of our decisions are made on this basis. In the story of our two climbers, Bernard may have decided that climbing in poor conditions was more important than being seen as a failure. I suspect that many people also decide that simply not taking on a challenge is more important than the risk of failing publicly. Others would say that giving it a go was more important.

Interestingly, many of the world-class performers that I've worked with, and studied, are not overly concerned with "success" and "failure". They tend to be happy to push the envelope and try new things, in the full realization that they'll probably fail. It is pretty normal to fail at something we haven't done before. If we step far enough outside of our comfort zone, we should probably expect to fail initially. Failure isn't a problem for many world class performers, because they were never motivated by a need to be seen as "successful". They are often happy to try, fail, learn, refine, try again, and so on. It is more important for them to become better today than they were yesterday, and better tomorrow than they are today.

It is pretty normal to
fail at something we
haven't done before.

When people contemplate challenges, they'll often find reasons not to embark upon them. Maybe it is "too expensive", or it will take "too much time". What they are actually saying is, "the money is more important than the challenge", or "I'd rather have the time". It doesn't take a genius to realize that high achievers are often single-minded and doggedly determined. They make decisions to put the achievements ahead of many other things in their lives. Elite business people, professionals, entrepreneurs and athletes all talk of the "sacrifices" they make to be successful. To phrase that slightly differently, they're saying that their challenge is so important to them, they have chosen to do without a lot of the things that others choose to keep. Some talk of the time they spend as a "sacrifice". They choose to spend time in pursuit of success, rather than spending their time doing other things. Often, this also means that they're making choices to put their achievements ahead of some relationships. In other cases, it means that they're choosing to accept a lower standard of living or reduced income. They may also decide to take some financial risks, or even risks with their health and wellbeing.

Robyn Benincasa made a conscious decision to keep going during the World Championships in Scotland, even though she'd blown her hip out and knew it meant another hip replacement (she's on her fourth). She also decided to use the last of her knee cartilage to help her finish a race, even though it meant literally moving her legs with her hands. It seems that, to Robyn, completing the challenge is more important than joints, bones and body parts.

You may wonder why I presented the word "sacrifice" in quote marks. To me, it is always a choice. Many world class performers recognize that their choices are positive. They have chosen to spend their time, money and energy in pursuit of their passion. When this happens, they are choosing to follow a certain path because they prefer to; not because they have to. If you were spending vast amounts of time doing something that you love, would you describe it as a "sacrifice"?

In some cases, however, people make negative choices. Those who are driven by a need to achieve the outcome, or who are motivated by a need to be recognized, may perceive that they're "sacrificing" something. In fact, they are likely to perceive that their time, energy or money is being spent on something in the hope and expectation that there will be a return. Rather than positively choosing something out of preference, they will make "sacrifices" in order to achieve the success they seek.

Striking the Balance

Single-mindedness is something that is often associated with high achievers. Often their tunnel-vision focus leads them to become selfish. In fact, many elite performers that I've come across openly admit to being incredibly selfish. As I stand here at the start of my challenge, I'm wondering if it is possible to achieve amazing feats without becoming ruthlessly single-minded and selfish. I don't want to become a selfish or single-minded person. I will not allow myself to become single-minded, because my life has too many things that are important to me. There are too many valuable things in my life that I'm not willing to sacrifice.

Even the most exciting and fulfilling challenges often have a cost associated with them. If, in taking on your challenge, you put at risk those things that mattered most dearly to you, I suspect you'd question whether it was ever worth it. My challenge will take a great deal of time, energy and determination, but if, in completing it, I damaged my marriage or my relationship with my children, I would cross the finish line and wonder what on earth I'd been doing. Quite simply, my wife and girls are far more important to me than a ridiculous endurance challenge. This challenge is important to me, but not important enough to risk my relationship with my loved ones. It is also not important enough to go bankrupt for. I realize that I'll need to invest a great deal of time, some money and gallons of sweat. I know that I'll have to make choices between sleep and training. I fully accept that I'm going to spend a lot of time feeling stiff, sore and tired. I am willing to put myself through discomfort and pain, but I'm not willing to impose that upon those around me.

In order for success to be sustainable, I believe that there has to be a balance. Kenny Atkinson is a great example of this. He is a twice Michelin-starred chef. Over the years, he has made some choices to work long and unsociable hours, take pay cuts and move to the far-flung corners of the country in order to become the best chef he can be. He hasn't done it alone. Kenny's wife has also been through these trials with him. She has also endured the hours, the tough financial times and the upheaval. Interestingly, at the Be World Class conference in 2012, Kenny talked about the need to invest as much into his relationships and his family as he does into his professional life. He realizes that there needs to be a balance.

What are you actually willing to "sacrifice" to achieve your goals, and what will you not sacrifice?

Decisions, Decisions

What are you willing to do in order to be successful?

There is an interesting little conversation that goes on between my ears when the alarm clock goes off. It's 5.15 am on a cold and dark December morning. My training schedule says "cycling", which means an hour in the garage on the turbo trainer. I don't know about your garage, but mine isn't the most luxurious place on a wet, cold, dark winter's morning. There is a temptation when that alarm clock goes off to hit the snooze button, or to switch it off or throw it across the room. As I hear the beeps, my brain starts to ask annoying questions. "Do I really need to get up? Could I do this later in the day? Is this session vital? If I decided to stay in bed, would it really make all that much difference?" It is in these moments that people decide whether they are actually willing to do what it takes to be successful. These are the choices that carve out our path. Do we opt for the warm, cosy, dry bed and drift back off to sleep? Or, do we haul ourselves out, put on our training kit and head out to the garage for an hour to watch the rain fall on the driveway? Most of the time, I make the decision to get up and head out, because training is more important than staying in bed. Sometimes I conclude that rest is more important and that I need to recover.

There is a context to my decisions. There are things that I am unwilling to do and things I choose not to do. Do I choose to spend a morning at home with my family at the weekend, or do a three- to four-hour training ride on the bike? Does the entrepreneur starting a new business buy new equipment if it means using the money that would otherwise be spent on a family holiday?

You'll no doubt face very similar choices and decisions. I always find it fascinating to see the impact that the "why" has on these apparently tiny choices. Ultimately, of course, it is the cumulative and compound effect of these seemingly small decisions that dictates our success.

What do we lose in order to gain "success"? Is it really worth it?

I would argue that our success is defined by the way in which we complete our challenges, not just by their completion alone.

Chapter Summary

* It's not enough to have a strong reason; you also need to have the right reason.
* Have you tested your motives? Which ones are central, and which are peripheral?
* What do your decisions tell you about your priorities? What is important to you?
* Are you motivated by a desire to be better today than you were yesterday, and better tomorrow than you are today?
* What are you willing to do to succeed, and what are you not willing to do?

Chapter 3
The How

"Nothing is impossible, the word itself says 'I'm possible'."

Audrey Hepburn

When most people embark upon epic challenges, I suspect they have no clue about how to achieve them. Let's be honest, if you're taking on a challenge that no one else has attempted, there is no blueprint. As I began explaining my challenge to the people around me, they would ask, "How on earth are you going to do that?" The only honest answer is, "I have no idea." When world class performers start out, they often have very few answers. What they do have is a head full of questions! These questions are the start point. They will help us to find the answers. However, the questions alone may not be enough. There is another, rather magical ingredient that gives real power to the process. It is the catalyst, the primer, the "fairy dust". What am I talking about?

Curiosity.

When we are curious, we have an intrinsic desire to find the answers. We actively search for solutions. Have you ever seen children who are powered by curiosity? They take on a terrier-like tenacity to explore and discover. If we have questions, but no curiosity, we'll probably get no further than the questions. If our questions go unanswered for too long, we may end up concluding that we simply can't proceed because we don't know the answers. Maybe we'll never find the answers. Perhaps this challenge is impossible after all. When we are curious, however, we keep searching until we find the solution.

> Some people simply don't accept the conventional barriers that most of us would. Student Scott Young decided he wanted an MIT (Massachusetts Institute of Technology) education but didn't want to go through the acceptance boards, get into debt or take four years over it. His curiosity led him to construct the entire four-year computer science and business curriculum, including the assessments, himself (Young, 2012).

Psychologist George Lowenstein (1994) described curiosity as a passion, "with all the motivational intensity that is implied by the term". Therefore, when we have that magical blend of questions and curiosity, we have a really good chance of finding some answers.

What are the big questions that you have at the moment? What do you need to know? How can you find the answers? Who could you ask? If they don't know, do they know someone that might know?

When we get into the flow, the process takes on a life of its own. Every answer that we find normally has another question that accompanies it. It becomes an adventure, like following the yellow brick road in *The Wizard of Oz*.

I wonder how I could do it?"

"You could ask someone!"

"Who might know?"

"They might know!"

"If they don't know, do they know
someone who might?"

Follow the yellow brick road!

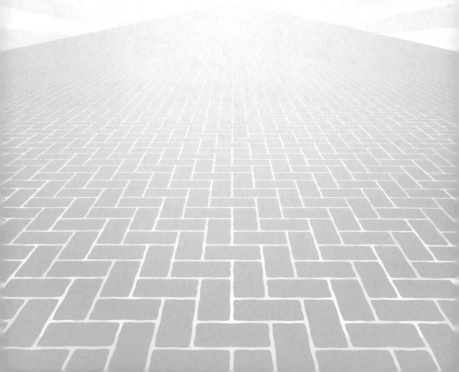

What if I Don't Find the "Right" Answers?

Good question. What if there are no "right" answers? What if there are only "different" answers? Undoubtedly, there are some answers that might be more effective than others. There will be some ways that are quicker than others. Some will give more complete solutions. However, it is also true that one solution does not fit all. The answer that is "right" for one person, may not be "right" for another.

When I work with soccer players, I often see coaches teaching skills to young players. Some coaches will show the players the "best" way to kick the ball. This "best" way often comes from the coaching manual. It is portrayed as the tried and tested, most efficient and effective way of kicking a ball. However, there is a problem. The players are all different. Some have longer legs than others. Some have bigger feet. Some have skinny legs, others are more muscular. Since the very first movements inside their mothers' wombs, they began to develop different neural networks in their brains. Therefore, the "best" way to kick a ball for one person is often very different from the "best" way for another.

What would happen if we allowed each of the players to find the way that worked most effectively for them? Rather than imagining that there was a right answer, could we simply encourage them to find different ways to kick a ball with control, accuracy and precision?

In fact, if you take any challenge, whether it is a physical challenge or not, there are a variety of different ways to approach it. Autobiographies of successful performers often illustrate that the journey to "the top" is often very different. Everyone has slightly different experiences and learns slightly different lessons along the way. There is no common start line. My life experience is different from yours. You will build on your knowledge and experience, and I'll build on mine. Therefore, it stands to reason that our "best" answers will probably be different as well.

As we progress through our challenge, the demands change and the questions change. Just when we start to make progress, and begin to feel like we know what we're doing, new questions appear, so the cycle starts all over again. It's a dynamic process, which constantly requires us to find new answers.

Take, for example, the question: how do you build a multi-million pound empire? One answer is to start by building a business that makes a few thousand pounds a year, and gradually grows to make tens, then hundreds of thousands, then millions. Having worked with entrepreneurs and business leaders, I have seen many of the transitions they go through. As their business grows, there are new challenges and demands. To meet these new demands, they find that they require new skills. For example, as they set out on their own as a sole trader, they need to learn how to run a business. All of a sudden they need to know about sales and marketing, finance, taxation, business planning, and so on. It soon becomes apparent that they need to find some experts around them, such as accountants and advisors. But how do you select these people? How do you know what a "good" accountant looks like?

As human beings, we learn a lot through trial and error. It's unlikely that we'll find the perfect solution first time. Normally, we'll refine as we go along and gradually get better. Just as many entrepreneurs have mastered these initial challenges, they find new ones. If our entrepreneur has started to become successful, they'll probably need to take on some staff. Now there's an interesting challenge! How do we know the best people to recruit? How do we lead them and manage them when they arrive? How do we feel about relinquishing some control and allowing them to make decisions about our business?

Of course, this process doesn't just apply to entrepreneurs and businesses. Musicians go through similar journeys as they progress from local performances in front of small gatherings of friends and family, to tens of thousands of people in theatres and arenas. Along the way, there are those slightly bigger venues with hundreds and then thousands of spectators. They also take on ever more complex and demanding pieces of music. The simple point is: we don't achieve these things overnight, or in one step.

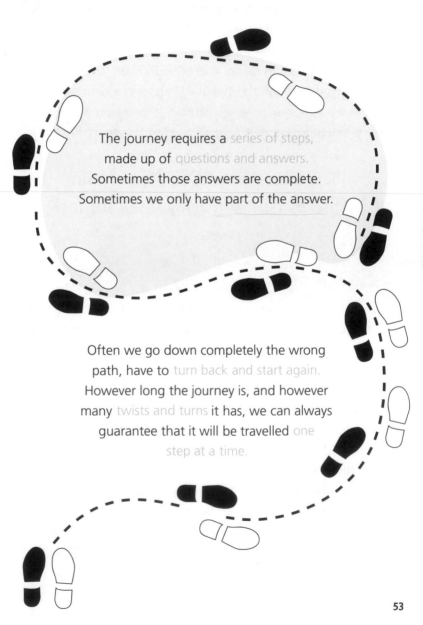

The journey requires a series of steps, made up of questions and answers. Sometimes those answers are complete. Sometimes we only have part of the answer.

Often we go down completely the wrong path, have to turn back and start again. However long the journey is, and however many twists and turns it has, we can always guarantee that it will be travelled one step at a time.

My experiences of working as a sport psychology coach also tell me that different personality types approach challenges very differently. Some people like to "think on the run". They are very happy to start off with a basic sketch outline and refine the plan as they go along, knowing that it will evolve. Others need far more detail before they begin. These people need to flesh out the plan and work through the "what if?" questions before they set off. Either way, in reality we all start off at the beginning and get there one step at a time.

> "The man who moves a mountain
> begins by carrying away small stones."
>
> *Confucius*

Using Our Discomfort Zone

Most of us spend most of our time operating in our comfort zone. We do things that are familiar, that we are comfortable and confident with. Some people actively step outside their comfort zone. In doing so, they often enter the unknown. It is something that I've seen elite athletes doing. The very best athletes have a good understanding of where their comfort zone ends and the discomfort zone begins. They also understand that they make the greatest improvements when they are in their discomfort zone.

I've noticed top athletes using their discomfort zone as a way of gaining constant improvements. They will set themselves a challenge that is outside their comfort zone. For example, they might want to hone a skill, or be able to apply that skill in a new way.

I once watched an international rugby player practising his kicking. He would start by setting himself a target area on the ground, using marker cones. Once he had his target, he would challenge himself to land the ball in that target 20 times in a row. If he missed one, he'd start again. He also made sure he could execute the skill with both feet. Once he'd landed 20 in a row, he'd make the target zone smaller and start again. As soon as he'd mastered that, he would get another player to pass him the ball before he kicked. He'd specifically ask that the passes were imperfect; some high, some low, some too short, some in front and some behind. Then, he would get one of his teammates to run at him so that he had less time and space. Each time, the skill became more difficult. As soon as he became comfortable, he changed the challenge and stepped back into his discomfort zone. His comfort zone would grow to encompass the new skills, and then he'd extend himself again.

So, why don't most of us do this? Why wouldn't we keep stepping outside of our comfort zone and strive to improve ourselves at every opportunity? Why is it that we tend to gravitate towards our comfort zone?

Here's one possible answer …

If we spent most of our time in our discomfort zone, we would spend a lot of time not being very good.

When we step into our discomfort zone we tend to make mistakes. It doesn't take a genius to work out that whenever we try something new, or more challenging, we also increase the chances that we'll screw up. If making mistakes also makes us feel bad, there's a good chance that we'll avoid doing it.

> It's not what happens that causes us the problems; it's how it makes us feel. More specifically, it's how we feel about ourselves.

If we start to view ourselves as "a failure" whenever we make a mistake, it's highly likely that we'll steer away from those situations. However, we don't have to make that mental link. If we perceive that making mistakes means that we are a failure, it is because we injected that meaning. It is our perception of mistakes, and failing, that causes us the angst.

What if we were happy pushing ourselves and stepping into our discomfort zone, knowing that we were likely to fail? What if we could accept the mistakes? What if we were happy knowing that other people might also see us try something and fail at it? Imagine if we didn't care about what they thought. Would you honestly rather try and fail, or not try at all?

If no one was watching,
what would you do?

A Tale of Two Sisters

Once upon a time there were two sisters, one aged six and the other five. As with many children of their age, these two bundles of loveliness were learning to ride their bicycles. Their daddy (that's me if you hadn't already worked it out) had taken the bold step of removing the stabilizers (a.k.a. training wheels). One sunny afternoon in May the two excited girls, and their rather nervous daddy, were out in the yard with the bicycles. Their epic mission: to ride on their own, without any help at all! Now that's quite a challenge.

Let me give you a little insight into the two sisters. Like many siblings, they are like chalk and cheese. Although their challenge was the same, their approach to it was very different. The slightly older of the two tends to be the quieter, calmer one. She also tends to listen and consider things before trying them out. In many ways, the younger sister is the more physically capable and athletic. As well as being physically strong, she is also strong willed and has a noticeable stubborn streak (which she gets from her mum – not me, honest). The youngest of the pair tends to be more impetuous. She prefers to get stuck in and try it first, rather than listening and considering. Sometimes this works for her, sometimes it doesn't.

As they started out, the two girls had a very similar

level of ability. They were both very wobbly and needed a lot of support to begin with. They took it in turns to ride along with daddy supporting them. Their daddy gave them exactly the same advice – keep peddling and steer. Neither of the sisters took to it straight away; they both tried, with varying degrees of success. One sister got upset when things didn't work out quickly. She started to get frustrated and irritated when she was offered advice. She didn't want to learn how to ride her bike, she just wanted to be able to do it.

The other sister approached things differently. She would give it a go and actively tried to follow the advice. Inevitably it wouldn't work first time, or second, but she would make a few changes and go again. Often she'd say, "oh, that was closer, I think I'm getting better" and "I almost did it". She was engaged in the process of learning and understood that she was making progress, however small. Unlike her younger sister, she didn't view this as "black and white", "all or nothing" or "success or failure". You will not be surprised to hear that after a little while she began to cycle independently. It was just a metre or so at first, but gradually became three metres, five metres, ten metres ... and she was off. "Daddy I can do it, I'm cycling on my own."

Those innocent words were like a red rag to a bull.

The fact that her older sister could now ride her bike made the younger one more determined to succeed. Unfortunately, her determination was also accompanied by impatience. She tried, didn't succeed, tried again and still didn't succeed. The younger sister was focused on the "black and white", the "all or nothing". She wasn't looking for glimmers of progress, so she didn't see them. As far as she could see, she had nothing and her sister had everything. She was trying again and again, but still had nothing. Her frustration compounded. After a few attempts she broke down in tears. "I'm the worst bike rider in the whole wide universe, and my bike is the worst bike ever." In her eyes she'd failed. She concluded that her sister was just better at riding a bike. It's almost as if her sister had received this amazing gift from on high, and she hadn't. "It's just not fair."

It's tough as a parent to see your beloved little ones tying themselves in knots, but it illustrates how differently humans take on challenges. It shows how our perceptions of success and failure impact upon us. It shows what happens when we focus on the process as opposed to outcomes, on progress rather than hard results. Are we engaged in the journey, or only interested in the destination? Can we celebrate "almost", or is that failure?

"A lot of people think, they're just better than me, they're faster, they're more talented. That's not true. They probably do have better processes, great coaching, nutrition, etc. Talent doesn't get you to the top and keep you there. That comes from years of doing the right things."

Robyn Benincasa, world record holder

Where Do I Start?

I've watched many people attempting to take on challenges. Often the hardest part is simply getting started. However, if you look at the footpath in front of you, you might think "That seems easy enough".

If you were standing at the foot of the mountain looking up at the peak, you might think, "Gulp. That's a huge mountain."

A few people have asked me, "How do you write a book? Where do you start?" The answer is pretty simple. I start with an idea and then throw some thoughts at a page. Initially they are pretty random, but after a while I start to make sense of them and put them into some kind of order. Eventually, after a little "wriggling and jiggling" (that's a technical term), I have a structure. I'll then start writing something, normally pretty rough and ready, which will then be edited until it looks half decent. Gradually, it starts to look a little bit more like a book.

I'll tell you what doesn't happen.

I don't have a blinding flash of inspiration whereby the fully formed book appears in my mind. I don't sit down at my PC and type out the finished manuscript from beginning to end in one perfect draft.

So, what's the answer to the question?
Where do you start?

Here. Now.

Start where you are. Start with what you do know.
Start with what you can do.
Start with questions. Identify the next step.
Focus on the next step.
Take one step at a time.

Andy Reid used his previous life experience to help him take on the challenge of learning to live life as a triple amputee:

"When I was young we were involved in a road traffic accident. Mum came off worst and eventually had to have her lower leg amputated. She managed to raise a family with it, so I thought 'I'm a soldier. I'm supposed to be tough. She did it, so I should be able to do this.'"

We all have something to build on; some experiences, some knowledge, some previous skills. It may only be tiny, but invariably there will be something. If we look for what we "do" have, we're likely to find that "something".

> If we look for what we "do" have, we're likely to find that "something".

When I started my training for this challenge, I was running approximately three miles, two or three times a week. I found that I was often quite stiff and sore for a day or so after a run, and had started to believe that my body wasn't up to running on consecutive days. I thought that my body probably just needed a rest day in between runs. However, if I wanted to run from Land's End to London at the end of my challenge, I was going to need to run 35 miles per day for 10 consecutive days.

At the very beginning of my training programme, I decided that I needed to start running back-to-back days. I started with a 4.5 mile run one Saturday morning. It was a fairly steady pace and took me 35 minutes, which is just under eight minutes per mile. As expected, I woke up slightly sore and tired on the Sunday. Despite the slight discomfort, I decided to pull my trainers on and go for a run. I did two miles and it took me 18 minutes, which is nine minutes per mile. I felt like I was crawling around and it was exhausting. The following day I got up, feeling really tired, and ran 2.5 miles. It wasn't quick, or pretty, but I did it. I had broken my duck.

> "If you believe that you need to have
> all the answers before you can begin,
> the chances are you won't begin."

If you don't know the answer to your questions, one option is to ask.

If you don't know the answer to your questions, one option is to ask.

"I'll never succeed without a team"

This was a comment that former SAS Major, Floyd Woodrow, said to me when we were discussing world-class leadership during an event. He wasn't just referring to leading an SAS unit in combat operations though. To be successful in life, we all require a team around us. Even individual athletes have teams of people around them. If you watched footage of the London 2012 Olympic Games, you may have noticed many of the athletes crediting their team. That's not just modesty talking. Most athletes realize how important their team of coaches, sport scientists, physiotherapists, performance advisors and sport psychologists are. In fact, the very best athletes often develop a skill set that helps them to succeed. They become very good at leading and managing their teams, to get the very best from them.

"Don't just pick your friends. You need to find the right people. I found the people who were winning and who were in the winning teams. I looked at their strengths and identified what you need in order to be successful. You need world class people who understand synergy."

Robyn Benincasa, world record holder, on the importance of finding the right team

Perhaps a good starting point is to find a team of people. Who would be in your "dream team"? Who could help you to navigate your way through your challenges?

It's Like Navigating in a Fog

It can be a bit disconcerting sometimes, like navigating in poor visibility. Often we can only see the step right in front of us. Beyond the next step, it all looks a bit hazy. Have you ever noticed that, however foggy it gets, you can always see something? Even if it is just a few inches in front of you, there is always something. If you walk forwards, you'll see something else appear; something new. If we keep walking as far as we can see, we find that miraculously we never hit a solid wall of fog. There is always just a little bit more to see. The same is true when we take on challenges.

What would you do if you were driving and you encountered dense fog? I suspect that you'd slow down. The same mentality often applies to challenges. There are times when we may have good visibility. We might know exactly what we need to do and can see quite a long way ahead of us. As we feel more confident, we'll probably start to speed up. On other occasions, we might feel that we need to slow down. We might need more answers or need to spend more time checking our bearings.

That all seems pretty reasonable and straightforward, I'm sure you'll agree. However, we humans tend to complicate it. I can remember encountering fog when driving. Sometimes I am happy to simply slow down and be patient. Sometimes I get frustrated because I have somewhere to be and this blasted fog is going to make me late. I know I need to slow down but I don't really want to. The complication often comes when we add something else into the agenda. In this case, I don't want to be late. This obviously conflicts with the need to be patient.

Who would be in your "dream team"? Who could help you to navigate your way through your challenges?

If we have a challenge, and have set ourselves a deadline, we could start to get anxious or frustrated if we don't think we're making progress quickly enough. We start to get concerned that we're not going to achieve the outcome or the results. In this situation, we tend to start feeling "pressure". We need things to happen now. We need the answers now. What's going to happen if we don't find a solution? We start to imagine what will happen if we fail.

How will we look? What will others think? All of a sudden our challenge could start to look a little impossible.

Let's change the mental landscape slightly. Let's forget the outcome for a moment. I'm back in the car, driving to my meeting, when I encounter dense fog. Rather than focusing on being late, could I simply focus on driving safely? What's the problem with being late anyway? Am I concerned about what the person I'm meeting may think about me? Will they think I'm slovenly and unprofessional? Do I think that lateness equates to sloppiness? If I pride myself on being prompt, is the opposite also true? Maybe I need to challenge some of these perceptions and allow myself to be more patient. Perhaps a quick phone call to the person I'm meeting, explaining that I'm likely to be late, is the better response.

My brother, Jon, described similar feelings when he was trying to learn German.

"What was I going to do? I was failing at my homework; I wasn't picking it up. I was worried that I couldn't pick it up at the speed I needed to. It is a problem when you set goals for yourself and you can't seem to achieve them in the time needed. That's when the doubts creep in."

Taking on challenges inevitably means that we'll encounter uncertainty and the dreaded unknown. It means that we need to be more comfortable navigating in "the fog". It probably means that we need to become more patient, and less concerned with artificial timeframes, results and outcomes. Therefore, we may have to change our mental landscape.

Hey, Stop Moving the Goal Posts!

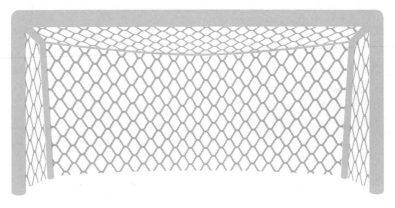

"Change is the only constant in life."

Heraclitus (approx. 500 BC, give or take a few days)

Have you noticed that things have a habit of changing? It is also true when taking on challenges. We humans tend to like certainty. In fact, many of our personal development "gurus" would suggest that we have a plan, set our course and head for it. Stephen Covey said, "Start with the end in mind."

Whilst there is nothing wrong with that philosophy per se, we do need to bear in mind the context we're working in. Life has a way of throwing us curve balls. Sometimes the "end" we have in mind isn't fixed. Often our route to getting there requires some flexibility. Challenges, like life, are fluid and dynamic. Even if our destination doesn't change, we may need to change course a few times to get there. I have heard world class performers describe the process as "tacking", like you'd do in a yacht. Although you may have a fixed destination, changes in winds, tides and currents mean that you constantly need to change course. Sometimes these might only be slight adjustments. On other occasions they may be significant. Often, our original plans need to be revised and updated. The time frame may shift, or the resources at our disposal might change. Essentially, we need to expect the unexpected. We need to expect that everything will not go to plan. As Heraclitus said, that's the only thing we can confidently predict.

Chapter Summary

- ★ When people embark on challenges, they often have no idea how they will achieve them.
- ★ Start with questions and curiosity; build on what you do know and can do.
- ★ The "right" answer for one person is often different from the "right" answer for someone else.
- ★ Are you happy making mistakes and failing? If no one was watching, what would you try?
- ★ Expect change and uncertainty, because it's the only thing you can confidently predict.

Chapter 4

Diving into Your Discomfort Zone

"Continuous effort – not strength or intelligence – is the key to unlocking our potential."

Winston Churchill

There is a very good reason why I keep referring to my endurance challenge as "ridiculous" and "daft". It is utterly bonkers. The point is, exceptional can never be normal. The word exceptional indicates that it's way outside of the norm. In my closing address at the Be World Class conferences in 2012, I reflected that world class people are often eccentric. A friend of mine reminded me of the meaning of the word eccentric a little while ago; it means "off centre". The dictionary defines eccentric as "departing from a recognized, conventional, or established norm or pattern" and "one that deviates markedly from an established norm, especially a person of odd or unconventional behaviour". Hmm, odd and unconventional behaviour … do I like the sound of that or not?

If you want to
achieve something
exceptional,
"normal" just
doesn't cut it.

Of course, there is a very good reason that world class people are eccentric. They are not normal. If they were normal, they would do normal things and they'd achieve what the rest of us achieve. The fact is, if you want to achieve something exceptional, "normal" just doesn't cut it.

Some people would shy away from the prospect of being abnormal or sticking out. They actively like to fit in. Far from wanting to be eccentric, they deliberately look to blend into their surroundings. For some people, departing from the norm is actually a pretty courageous step in itself. Those who are not considered "normal" can sometimes be the subject of ridicule. Unfortunately, the media have a habit of making the judgements. They seem to focus on those eccentrics that will be adored and those who are ridiculed.

In his book, *Outliers*, Malcolm Gladwell (2008) described the way that "cultural legacies", social attitudes and accepted norms can influence how we see people. Making the decision to abandon normality often requires us to be genuinely happy being ourselves. I often reflect on the world class performers that I've met. None of them do normal things, which of course is why they've achieved greatness. Many of them have made decisions that appear to be completely ludicrous. Polar explorer, Ben Saunders, gave up a "sensible" and "safe" career pathway as an officer in the British Army. Instead, he chose a career pathway that really didn't exist. Mountaineer, Alan Hinkes, gave up a "solid" profession in teaching to follow his passion and become a full-time mountaineer. What would their careers teachers have said?

It's time to depart from normality. Normal rules do not apply.

"That's Mental"

How many times have I heard those words when I've described my endurance challenge to other people? If I had a pound for every time … (I'm starting to sound like my dad).

Of course, there is a temptation that I could start to buy into the enormity of the challenge if I start to see it through other people's eyes. I remember describing my morning to a friend recently. I told him that I'd started my day by getting up, running a half-marathon, grabbing some breakfast, dropping the kids at school and then hitting the office. To him, this just seemed incredible. How could someone just get up and run a half-marathon before getting into the office? To me it wasn't particularly epic. Sometimes I'd run five to ten miles on a morning. Sometimes I'd run a little farther. This particular morning I had a bit more time so I ran a bit farther. Clearly his perspective and mine were very different. If you allow yourself to take on other people's perspectives, you may become limited by what they believe is possible or sensible.

I wonder how many of the world's great inventors or creators have heard the words, "it simply can't be done", or "that's impossible, you'll never do it, you're wasting your time". Did anyone ever tell Thomas Edison that perhaps, after 9000 failed attempts, he ought to give up on this daft "light bulb thingy" of his? The history of the world shows us countless examples of people that have been the first to break new ground. These people have turned the "impossible" into the "possible". I am sure that they were also told they were "mental" for attempting their hare-brained scheme.

How do you tend to respond if other people tell you that you're being daft or that it's not possible? Do you buy into their way of thinking and take on their perspective? Or do you smile and carry on your own way? It's often enlightening to reflect upon how much other people's thoughts, beliefs and perspectives impact on our own.

Could I Already Do This?

As I began training for my challenge, a realization began to dawn on me. Initially I thought that I was getting physically fitter and that my training was developing my physiology. As a student of sport and exercise science, I remember learning about how the body adapts to training; how it becomes more efficient at using oxygen, how muscles become stronger, etc. However, as I began to increase my mileage I started to question just how much of my progress was actually due to physiological changes. If I ran three miles one week and did six miles the week after, had my fitness doubled in a week? Or was there another, simpler, explanation? Did I have the capacity to run six miles all along? Was I actually training my mind to believe that it could run six miles?

As I have been training, I've taken the opportunity to engage in some self-reflection. I'm pretty sure that the primary effect of my training is simply confidence building. As a sport psychology consultant, I know that confidence is built on evidence. If I asked you to tie your shoe laces, how confident would you be? I'm guessing you'd be very confident. I suspect you'd even be confident that you could do it with your eyes shut. You've done it many times before, so you have a bank of evidence telling you that you're well capable of tying your shoe laces. What if I asked you to perform open heart surgery? If you happen to be a cardiac surgeon, that might not be too daunting. If you're not, I suspect you're not going to feel too confident.

Let's apply this mindset to running. If I have just run three miles and finished fairly strongly, I will probably feel pretty confident that I could do four miles, or even 4.5 miles. If I do the 4.5 miles okay, it's likely that I will see six miles as an achievable distance. As I keep building my distance, and finishing with a little bit left in the tank, I also build the belief that I could go a little farther. On the day that I ran 26 miles, I began to see that running 35 miles in a day was possible. Many of those who have taken on epic challenges talk of the "new horizons" that appear. As you hit the peak that you've been striving for, more possibilities present themselves and more of your potential becomes visible.

In truth, I can't tell you exactly how much of my progress is due to changes in my physical fitness. No doubt my body has adapted. However, I also suspect that much of my progress can be explained as "mental fitness": my confidence to use the capacity that was already there.

As double Olympic champion, Steve Williams, told me that belief was his biggest challenge. Initially he struggled to relate what he saw in others (such as Olympic legends Steve Redgrave and Matthew Pinsent) to the way he perceived himself.

"I don't feel the way I think they look. They look like machines and I don't feel like one."

I heard a piece of advice on the radio recently. It went something like this ...

"Don't compare your inside with
other people's outsides."

Boundaries and Milestones

As we learn something new, or take on a new challenge, we inevitably pass milestones. There are targets that once seemed like distant dreams, which all of a sudden look realistic and attainable. What once was tough, now seems comfortable. It's really interesting to understand the change in perspective that occurs when we start to develop. I often talk to athletes that are making the transition from one level to the next. They could be stepping up from national to international level, or from junior to senior level. It is the same for many professionals who take on new responsibilities, get higher targets, more staff or bigger budgets. In the early stages, it feels like we're out of our depth. It's unfamiliar. We're out of our comfort zone. In fact, we're slap bang in the middle of our discomfort zone. For some people, this can be a scary prospect. We could feel out of control.

Over the years I have worked with a number of elite athletes in motor sports, both on two wheels and four wheels. When they step up from one level to the next, they often find themselves in more powerful vehicles, which go much faster. In the early stages, this can be quite a challenge. When they're travelling faster, the corners come at them more quickly and the race track starts to look like a blur. If they're not careful, they could start to feel rushed, out of control and start to panic. They may not make great decisions to start with, and they are more likely to make errors. There is also a danger that all of this could get compounded if they make some noticeable mistakes early on.

Part of the challenge, for the racing driver, is to hone their focus. They need to be able to focus earlier, which gives them a greater sense of time, and helps them to make better decisions. This might all seem quite obvious in motor sport, but the same kinds of challenges exist for many of us when we step into new territory. Professional people may also have to make decisions quicker, they may have to focus on different things, analyse new information or consider more variables. All of this could seem overwhelming.

There is a potential that we could get ourselves caught up in a negative spiral if we make some mistakes, start to doubt ourselves, lose confidence and then make some more mistakes. Equally, there is an opportunity for us to recognize the new challenges, become aware of our progress (however small), appreciate the lessons we're learning and use this to build our confidence. Gradually we become acclimatized to the new demands and therefore perceive them as less daunting.

Date: A very cold day in November.

I spent a day on the river in a kayak. I'd asked Claire O'Hara (who just happens to be a world freestyle kayak champion and a great coach) if she'd help me learn how to paddle in moving water. There's a real skill in being able to read the water, the flow and the currents. I wanted to be able to learn how to work with the flow of the water, rather than battling against it.

You may remember me mentioning that I'm a novice in the kayak. My greatest skill is my ability to capsize the boat, even in the calmest of waters. It is something that I'm particularly adept at.

I knew, from tracking the weather and river conditions, that this particular stretch of river had been in flood just 24 hours beforehand. In fact, it was touch and go whether we should brave the conditions or not. As I turned up on the river bank, I saw a torrent of racing white water before me. My heart leapt into my mouth. Surely there was no way that I'd survive for more than a few seconds in there. Added to that, the air temperature was a touch below freezing and the water didn't look much warmer.

Despite being convinced that I was not going to stay afloat for more than a few nano-seconds, we took to the water. Claire found a patch of "slack" water and we got going. To my amazement I managed to control the boat. Gradually, Claire took us closer and closer to the main flow. I started to feel the way the water moved the boat. I began to predict where and how the boat was affected and what to do. Before the end of the day we paddled into the main flow of the river and rode the waves before coming back to the shore. Of course, it didn't stop me falling out of my boat and into the ice cold water, but I survived. More importantly, I have learned that I can control a boat in moving water!

How do you tend to respond when you're outside of your comfort zone? Do you find yourself panicking or honing your focus on the job in hand?

Use Your Discomfort Zone

You don't need me to remind you that we grow and improve when we're in our discomfort zone. However, there is another very useful realization that comes with this. When we find things that we're uncomfortable with, we become aware of the boundary; the point at which our comfort zone ends and our discomfort zone begins. Therefore we start to learn where and how we can make our greatest strides forward. Recognizing this discomfort helps to illuminate the very things we need to be doing.

One evening I was sitting on my living room floor, holding a kayak paddle handle. There was a good reason for this strange (let's call it eccentric) behaviour. The first time I sat in the kayak I noticed that I got cramp in the tops of my thighs, around the area of my hips. You can't simply get out of the boat and give them a stretch when you're several hundred metres from the shore. So, to stop myself getting cramp I decided to train these muscles. Io do so, I would replicate the position by sitting with my legs straight out in front of me on the living room floor. To help me practise my stroke, I had acquired a piece of the paddle handle.

When I first tried this rather bizarre exercise, I could just about manage three minutes, which were incredibly uncomfortable. My legs and my lower back were begging me to stop and jump back onto the sofa. The very fact that it was so uncomfortable convinced me that I needed to do more of it. All of a sudden I became aware of my discomfort zone and the need to step into it. Within a few weeks I was doing 30 minutes on the floor, then 45 minutes, then an hour plus.

Once we experience discomfort we have a choice: to approach it and engage it, or to back away. We definitely have an opportunity to use the discomfort to our advantage. We can choose to take those small steps away from what we can do, towards the things we can't yet do.

> We definitely have an opportunity to
> use the discomfort to our advantage.

When you encounter the boundary between your comfort zone and your discomfort zone, do you tend to stride into discomfort or gravitate back into comfort?

Baby Steps

I'd argue that the words "overnight success" are actually a complete misnomer. None of the people I have ever come across achieved anything "overnight", other than a good night's sleep. Many athletes seem to come from nowhere and just appear on the world stage. Of course, the reality is much different. Their "overnight success" takes years and years of work to achieve. When they emerge onto a world stage, it seems like an enormous leap. However, in their journey, it's actually just another relatively small step. Although they might be the new kid on the block as far as the media are concerned, they have probably been on the verge of the world stage for a long time.

In her book, *Bigger, Better, Bolder, Faster,* Kerrianne Cartmer-Edwards (2013) describes Albert Einstein's journey to becoming a genius. Although he is recognized as one of the greatest scientists of modern times, his start point was rather more modest. He graduated from Zurich Polytechnic with an unspectacular record and found it hard to pick up work as a teacher. Rather than becoming a researcher, young Albert took a job in the Patent Office and spent his leisure time reading, researching and writing scientific papers. Albert Einstein completed his PhD at the age of 26, whilst still working at the Patent Office, but had to wait a further year before the scientific community took notice of his work. Amazingly, it was eight years after first publishing his "General Theory of Relativity" that his findings were confirmed by other academics. It was as a result of this turn of events that Einstein was awarded his Nobel Prize.

Andy Reid described the process of learning to walk on his prosthetic legs.

"I would start by walking between the bars, just a few metres at first. Then I'd venture outside of the bars. Gradually I managed a little bit more and a little bit more. Week by week it built up."

Andy McMenemy once described his 66 ultra-marathons as "3.3 million strides", taken one at a time.

If we see our challenge as a series of baby steps, it is also possible that we start to realize that each of the steps is relatively simple.

Chapter Summary

★ If you want to achieve something exceptional, "normal" simply doesn't cut it.

★ If you allow yourself to buy into other people's perspectives, you could become limited by what they believe is possible.

★ Don't compare your inside to other people's outsides.

★ Use your experiences of discomfort to find ways to get better.

★ Overnight success never happens overnight.

Chapter 5
Taking Control

"Many of life's failures are people who did not realize how close they were to success when they gave up."

Thomas A. Edison

So far we've been looking at how to approach the challenge, how to get your head around those things that look "daunting", "enormous" and "impossible". How do we perceive the challenge? Are we willing to step beyond what we know? Can we push ourselves to do more than we thought possible? These are the conversations that we can engage in when we have a following wind and things are going reasonably well. It's been that viewpoint you can take more easily when things are good.

But what happens when things don't go well? What happens when we hit real hurdles? What happens when the smelly stuff hits the fan?

Many years ago I was listening to a successful entrepreneur describing how he'd made his millions. He explained that he had been successful in everything he had done. Listening to his story, I thought that this man must have had the Midas touch. Perhaps he had some special skills or knowledge that made him so successful. I wondered what he had that I didn't. Having read the autobiographies of successful athletes, entrepreneurs and personal development "gurus", I've seen many accounts of people that have gone from rags to riches. They all seem to be textbook success stories. These people come across as serial achievers. I have also heard professional speakers stand on stage explaining that they are winners, and will make sure they win at everything they do. They are the single-minded, determined types that have never quit and will never quit, because quitting is for losers. They simply don't accept failure.

Well here's the problem ... that's not me. I am not a serial success story. I'm a "b" grade student. I don't have a glowing track record. My CV doesn't show a steady stream of commercial successes and I certainly don't have the Midas touch. My history is a little more ... (let's think of a way of putting this politely) ... modest. I am a slightly overweight, thirty-odd-year-old with dodgy knees and a low pain threshold. I wouldn't describe myself as an insanely positive thinker either. To be honest, I don't believe in positive thinking. I am a realist. I'm not a superhero. I am just a fallible human.

Does this sound familiar? What can you do if it all goes wrong?

The Battle Between Your Ears

There's a constant mental tug of war that goes on between my ears. The contest is usually instigated by a doubt that appears in the form of a question.

Just this afternoon I ran through the delightful country lanes near my home. It was great to be out; the sun was shining, the birds were singing. It's been the kind of English spring day that we don't get often enough. A mile or so into my run I started to feel instability in my right knee. A few days ago I went for a run during the evening and my right knee completely seized up. Sharp pain shot down the inside of my knee and into my shin. I ended up walking home. Now I could feel it again, nagging at me. Should I keep going or call it quits and give it some rest? Am I just being a wimp? Surely those "mentally tough" individuals would just bulldoze through the pain and get on with it. Should I keep going or am I being stupid? Am I going to do myself damage by trying to run through the pain? I'm pretty sure that there is a reason for pain. Isn't it there to warn you that you're doing damage and persuade you to stop?

I kept trotting along, nursing my knee. Gradually, it began to feel more "normal". Often it takes two to three miles to get going when I'm doing a longer run. Maybe this was just my body settling into it.

A few minutes later my left knee began to tighten up, followed quickly by cramp in my right foot. "Oh great; what now? Come on body, you're supposed to be on my side." As I kept plodding along I started to question myself further. Am I really cut out to run 35 miles per day for 10 consecutive days? Here I am struggling to run 10 miles comfortably. My knee seized up within two miles a few days ago, so what chance have I got? Am I just being stupid?

Does any of this resonate with you?

Am I really cut out for this?

It is a question I ask myself a lot. Of course, a serial achiever will always say, "yes". Superheroes can do anything. I can hear the words ringing in my ears, "I always achieve whatever I set out to do." Is that actually true? Are there people in this world that have never set themselves a target and missed it? Am I the only one that sets out with a target in mind and falls short sometimes? Some days I will set myself an ambitious target, aiming to cover a specific distance within a training session and I'll limp home a mile or so short. Some days I have set myself a modest target and completely run out of gas halfway around. I will end up crawling home from a session that should have been quite "easy". It is often in these moments that my mind starts to ask the question … Are you sure you're cut out for this? Do you really have what it takes?

So how do you answer the part of your brain that doubts? Personally, I don't think that it can be fooled. My own mind seems to know me too well; it knows that I'm not a walking success story. It also knows that I don't have a track record to fall back on and that I don't have any previous experience of endurance challenges.

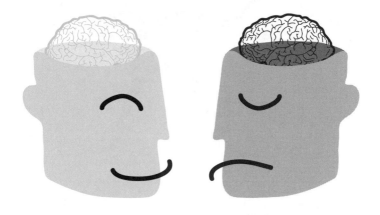

Just saying "I can do it, I can do it, I am the greatest" doesn't seem to cut it. My doubting brain just chuckles back at me and asks, "Who are you trying to fool?"

Earlier I mentioned that confidence is built on evidence. That is one thing that my doubting mind cannot argue with. One evening I hit "the wall" whilst I was running. It's a weird sensation. My energy levels crashed, my legs felt like jelly and I had this intense urge to just stop running, sit down and eat. The problem was, I had only got half way through my run. The urge to stop was all the greater because I was passing my house as I completed the first of two laps. Unlike the instability in my knees, I concluded that I wasn't likely to do any damage if I kept on running, so I decided to get my head down and plough on. The second lap was not very impressive, but I got round and finished. It wasn't a record-breaking, or particularly monumental achievement, in itself. However, it provides me with the evidence that when I hit "the wall" I can keep going for a few miles at least. It also teaches me that it's only a "wall" if I decide that's what it is. My perception gives it solidity. I'm the one that chooses whether to stop or to carry on.

> "The brick walls are there for a reason.
>
> The brick walls are not there to keep us out. The brick walls are there to give us a chance to show how badly we want something. Because the brick walls are there to stop the people who don't want it badly enough. They're there to stop the other people."
>
> *Randy Pausch*

I'm sure you'll have had similar experiences yourself. They ask interesting questions of us and present us with choices. How do you respond when you find your "walls"?

Winning the Battle

So, how do you start to turn the conversation around in those moments of doubt? How is it possible to win the tug of war against the doubting mind?

In the movie, *Any Given Sunday*, American football coach Tony D'Amato (played by Al Pacino) addresses his team at half time in their big game. His team are having a nightmare and they are getting thumped (pardon the technical term). So, Coach D'Amato delivers his half-time pep talk, popularly known as "the inches speech". It's an iconic motivational speech and one that many sports teams have seen over the years. He explains that football, like life, is a game of inches. To be successful, we need to fight for every inch. In his words, "The inches we need are all around us. They're in every break of the game, every minute, every second."

Coach D'Amato is saying that we don't need a magic wand. We don't have to look for the "silver bullet"; the one big thing that is going to turn all of this around. We don't need a miracle. He's telling his team that they don't need to win the game in the next play. Instead, they simply need to focus on each moment and do everything they can to find the next inch. He also reminds us that the opportunities we need are all around us, in every minute and second of our lives. Sometimes we simply need to open our eyes and look for them.

I have found that mentality to be incredibly helpful in all sorts of different ways. It has helped me to get on top of debts. It is tempting to think that you can only clear off a big debt if you happen to receive a big cheque. This is especially true when you're also finding it hard to make the income you do have stretch far enough.

the opportunities we need

are all around us,

in every minute

and second of our lives

The idea of using any of this scarce resource to pay off debts seems daft. But, of course, this leaves us in a "catch 22" where the debts keep rising and are ever more daunting. However, there is another way of looking at it. By simply replacing the word "inch" with "pound" (or dollar, euro, etc.) we find another way of climbing out of debt. Our brains are great at solving problems, as long as we ask them the right questions. How could I find an extra one pound in my weekly budget to reduce my debts? In sport we often look for ways to shave a tenth of a second from a performance, or add a few centimetres. The easiest way to find a tenth of a second is to find one hundredth of a second ten times. This approach is easily applied to any challenge. The easiest way to find ten pounds is to find one pound ten times. The easiest way to find an extra pound is to find ten pence ten times. Try it with your challenge and see how much extra you can find.

This mentality isn't limited to physical challenges. My brother, Jon, applied a similar approach when he was struggling to grasp the German language. He started by going around the city reading signs and posters and things. He did simple things like order a cup of tea or buy a train ticket and gradually built up his confidence.

Andy Reid explained that the challenge of walking again used to seem daunting. The only way he could engage with it was to break it down and focus on the step right in front of him.

"Whenever things got tough, I looked for little goals. I wanted to go to the Remembrance Day service in 2009 with my company. The doctor told me that I had to get out of my wheelchair, to the floor and back up before he'd let me go. Having been given the challenge, that was good enough for me. I was in the physio room the next morning."

In order to find these inches, we simply need to look for them. Where are your next inches?

Just One Inch at a Time

A few years ago I travelled to Madeira on holiday. It is a beautiful island, but incredibly steep. Madeira is essentially the peak of a mountain, sticking out of the Atlantic Ocean. One morning I decided to run up to the top of the hill where we were staying. It was a long, steep and winding climb to the top. I put my head down and started plodding. It didn't take long before my legs and lungs began to burn. I was panting, sweating and just staring at the ground as I plodded slowly up the hill. At one point I made the mistake of looking up to see how far I had to go. I obviously hadn't run as far as I thought. There was still an awful lot of hill left to go and I was already knackered. The doubts came flooding through my mind. They were exactly the same questions that I find invading my thoughts today. Can I do this …? Am I cut out for this …?

In the absence of a new set of legs, or lungs, I decided to adopt the "inches" approach. I saw a pebble on the road a few metres ahead of me. I said to my legs, "Come on legs, I am not asking you to get to the top but can you get to the pebble?" I made it to the pebble. As I got close to the pebble my eyes scanned a few metres ahead to a small bush on the verge of the road. "Come on legs, can you make it to the bush?" Gradually, small stride after small stride, inch by inch, my very tired legs and lungs carried me up the hill … to the very top. It's something I do quite often when I am training now.

"Steve [Redgrave] spoke very openly about his doubts, about tough races, about not knowing if he could do another 10 strokes. I thought, 'He's just like me. He gets nervous. He doubts. He wasn't born different. He's not immune to human responses. He's a champion because he can deal with them. Everyone has to learn it and it can be learned.'"

Steve Williams, OBE, double Olympic gold medallist

There is a myth about Olympic champions and world record holders: that they have cast iron self-belief and that negative thoughts don't enter their heads. We might even think that we are different from these people because we do have doubts and negative thoughts, and it is these that hold us back.

Even the very toughest people, like adventure racer Robyn Benincasa, have doubts. She openly revealed that her mind also raises these same issues, "I don't know if I can hold this together." Her answer is to ask a question in return. "But can you take the next step and then the next? ... as long as you can keep moving forward there is always a way." World champion and Olympic bronze medal winning triathlete, Jonny Brownlee, told me that when he stands on the pontoon before diving into the water at the start of a race he often thinks, "What if I can't swim?"

It's tempting to think that having doubts equates to weakness. Clearly these accounts show that even Olympic champions and world record holders have doubts. Doubting doesn't show that we're weak; it shows we're human.

Is That SMART or DUMB?

As my knees were aching just this afternoon, I was reflecting on the mental wrestle and listening to the conversation in my brain. Ironically it struck me that I was engaged in a form of "SMART" goal setting. I was breaking down my challenge into "specific", "measurable", "achievable" and "realistic" chunks. Maybe I had been too hasty in judging those SMART goals after all. Perhaps there is a place for the DUMBER and the SMARTER processes. World class performers typically focus on the next step; the one right in front of them. They are very aware of the end goal, but they don't spend a great deal of time focusing on it. Instead, they bring their focus back to the moment they are in and the task at hand. In doing so, they also simplify the job and give themselves an infinitely greater chance of executing it really well.

So, is it possible for SMARTER and DUMBER goal setting to live happily together? Can we have "daft", "bonkers" and "unrealistic" goals as well as "specific", "measurable" and "achievable"? What if our "why" was based on DUMBER goals? What if our imagination was allowed to run wild, in the way that Walt Disney's mind did when he conceived the idea for his fairy-tale princess castle in the middle of a swamp? If we let our minds run free, without the need for sensible, SMART thinking, what would we dream up? How exciting would that be?

Once we have our DUMBER goals, we need to find a way to help us get there. Maybe this is where those SMARTER goals could come in handy. Maybe they help us with the "how". Perhaps they are a way of helping us to understand the "inches" and allowing us to focus on "the next step".

Those Serial Success Stories

I have a theory. I don't think that I am the only one who sets out to do something and falls short. I also suspect that when we read, or hear, of the wall-to-wall success stories, we're not getting the whole picture. I don't think that they're lying; I just feel that we're getting the edited version with the murky bits removed. For almost 20 years I have worked with and studied a wide range of elite and world class performers. To date I haven't seen one that has been completely successful at their first attempt. Most of them have more than their fair share of failures and they tend to make plenty of mistakes.

I recently read an article by Simon Sinek (2010) about the legendary baseball player, Babe Ruth. In 1923, Babe Ruth broke the Major League Baseball record for the most home runs and the highest batting average in a season. However, there is a third record that many people are not aware of. In the same season, Babe Ruth was also struck out more times than any other player in the league.

Babe Ruth was not afraid to strikeout. Arguably, it was this fearlessness that contributed to his remarkable career. He was the first player to hit 60 home runs in one season, a record he held for 34 years. He also held the lifetime total home run record of 714 for 39 years until Hank Aaron broke it in 1974. Babe Ruth held other records too. He had 1,330 career strikeouts – a record he held for 29 years until it was broken by none other than the great Mickey Mantle.

Most baseball players want to hit home runs. The problem is they are afraid to fail in order to get there. As Babe Ruth proved, you can't have one without the other. It's perfectly fine to be a good, solid player who doesn't go down swinging that often ... but it also means you're unlikely to hit that many home runs.

In itself, this characteristic is very interesting. The fact that people like Babe Ruth are willing to push the envelope, try new things and make mistakes, differentiates them from the people around them. However, the very best in the world also combine another powerful element. They have an uncanny knack of learning from every experience. Their mistakes and failures are valuable, because they squeeze every possible ounce of benefit from them. If I accept that I am going to have my own fair share of failures, the question is: What can I learn from them?

Chapter Summary

- ★ Even Olympic champions and world record holders have doubts.
- ★ Life, like football, is a game of inches. The inches we need are all around us.
- ★ Focus on the moment: break it down and simplify the task.
- ★ Don't be afraid to fail.
- ★ What can you learn from your mistakes and failures?

Chapter 6

It's Not Just About You

"The main ingredient of stardom is the rest of the team."

John Wooden

The people around us can have a powerful influence on us. Their feedback, their support, their encouragement, or indeed their doubts, all have the potential to shift our thinking and emotions. When I watch young athletes at work, I see some that have an incredibly supportive family. Their parents pick them up, drop them off and drive the lengths of the country taking them to training camps or competitions. Often these parents invest a huge amount of time and energy in their children.

Of course, not all of the influences are positive. How often do you see "pushy parents"? Their ambitions for the child can actually present other challenges. It is often a double-edged sword. I have worked with a lot of junior athletes who feel under massive pressure to meet the expectations of parents and coaches. Some youngsters feel that they need to repay all of the "investment" that their parents make through their performance and results.

Of course, this phenomenon is not confined to athletes. Parents have been known to push their children academically, in music, drama and according to the career choice that they aspire to on behalf of their offspring. Clearly, there are some influences that can be positive, and others that could be negative.

The Positive Energy

"If you want to be successful, surround yourself with positive people."

That sounds like good advice, doesn't it? Positive people are likely to be more encouraging and supportive. They say things like, "go for it" and "you'll be great". Supportive people tend to give you the kind of feedback that boosts you, or picks you up from a fall. They might just give you a lift if you're feeling low. I have heard many successful people describing the importance of having someone that believed in them. Equally, there are those who offer to help and those who provide the very real and tangible support that enables you to get things done.

Jon, my brother, found a network of people to support him as he established his new business in Germany. He sought out other like-minded professional people, talked through ideas, found that they shared some common thoughts and views, and decided to collaborate on projects together. He found it very energizing to work with others that shared his goals, passion and values.

In preparing for this daft endurance challenge, I've found some amazing people. Some have provided some much needed advice and knowledge. Others have offered to take time out to help coach me and help me develop skills. I am very grateful to John at Cyclesense who helped me get going on the bike, and Nigel Dennis from Sea Kayaking UK, who helped with the boat. Help and support of this kind is absolutely invaluable.

So, how do you manage to surround yourself with the kind of people that will provide this positive energy? I guess it's possible that some people may just find you and offer their help. However, I think the chances are quite slim. Personally, I have used the opposite approach. I tend to seek people, and ask for their help. For example, I asked Claire O'Hara (a freestyle kayak champion) to point me in the direction of the UK's most respected sea kayak expert. One of my friends and clients, Richard, is a keen cyclist and has completed some epic rides himself. He suggested I contact John at Cyclesense who offered to help me get going. I am very grateful for their assistance, advice and support.

There is also a wide range of people that either won't, or can't, provide support. I tend to find that they identify themselves fairly early on. They might not return calls or emails. They may say "no". Equally, they may say "yes" initially, but are then unable to help for some reason. Gradually, through a process of asking, talking and developing relationships, it's possible to create a team of people that help to propel you along.

Where can you plug into a healthy source of positive energy?

The Negative Energy

Sometimes the feedback and input from others is not positive. So, what do we do if we're bombarded by negativity?

Steve Williams faced this challenge in the lead up to the Beijing Olympic Games in 2008. His boat (the coxless four) was not the favourite and was not the flagship British boat. They had been beaten in the World Championship the year before and also in the World Cup series just a few weeks beforehand. The British delegates in the IOC (International Olympic Committee) had elected not to present the medals at their medal ceremony because it was felt they didn't have a great chance of winning. Steve read a newspaper report, which listed Great Britain's top 10 rowing gold medal prospects, and his crew weren't one of them.

Where can you plug into a healthy source of positive energy?

> "I thought, 'Screw you, we'll show you.' You can't control what others say, or think, or do, or whether they believe in you. You only choose how you respond."

Steve Williams, OBE, double Olympic champion and adventurer

Adventure racer, Robyn Benincasa, faced similar negativity during a race in Brazil. It was shortly after her second hip replacement and she was struggling. The team was split. Some members wanted to go on without her, whereas others viewed it as a team game.

"Some people would say that if they get to the finish line, as an individual, they're successful. I don't subscribe to that. This is a team game. If we get to the finish line, we're successful."

In the end they decided to go on together as a team and reach the next checkpoint. Then they simply kept going, working from checkpoint to checkpoint all the way to the finish.

Not all of the energy is going to be positive. There are likely to be those who have doubts or fears of their own. Often they are not intending to be "negative", they're just being honest. They don't set out to pull you back. We humans often find it difficult to stop ourselves expressing what we think and feel. When we are with the people closest to us, we might feel that we should be honest. In fact, we may feel like we should be honest, even if it's not what they want to hear. Therefore, ironically, a lot of the "negative" energy comes from those that are our nearest and dearest.

The Difficult Conversations

The first real test was the conversation I had with Caroline, my wife. Love presents a few challenges of its own. If I didn't care about what Caroline thought, this conversation would have been a breeze. I would simply have ignored any negativity or concerns and ploughed ahead regardless. I know many "single-minded" people that have achieved incredible feats, or built million pound businesses, at the expense of their marriages and families. The problem is, I have never been willing to do that. I love my wife and daughters far too much to do that. I've made the decision to sacrifice the speed of growth in my business so that I can spend time with my family, so I didn't want to jeopardize that.

When I first described the idea of this challenge to Caroline, her response was, "Absolutely not … no way …over my dead body". I'll be honest, that wasn't the outcome I was looking for. Needless to say, she didn't like the idea at all. She knew that it would mean that I'd need some time away from the family. It was going to place another strain on our already stretched finances. I was going to be putting myself at risk. As she reminded me, the North Sea is a dangerous place and I have absolutely no experience in a kayak. Even though this challenge was in aid of charity, she quite rightly pointed out that I was being incredibly selfish. The whole thing would place an enormous demand on us as a family and, quite frankly, she didn't see the point of it.

When I first mentioned it to my parents, they thought I was completely mad. My mum was horrified at the idea that I was planning to kayak over 800 miles up the coast of the North Sea. She asked some very sensible questions, like "What about the weather conditions, the tides, the sea conditions? What about your knees?" (I've had surgery on both knees). In fact, the more we talked the more unanswered questions we seemed to accumulate. With every unanswered question came more doubts and fears. There is no fooling the people who are closest to you and know you the best. My family knows that I am no athlete. They know that I am a slightly overweight thirty-something with dodgy knees, no experience of kayaking, no experience of distance running and no experience of cycling. On several occasions they asked the question, "Have you any idea what this entails?" My honest answer: "No, I don't! I genuinely have no concept of what it will take to do this."

The feedback from people closest to us can often have the greatest influence. Of course, we have a closer emotional connection to them so it is harder to simply ignore what they say. The very fact that we care about them means that we can't simply detach ourselves. I have also noticed that whenever I take on challenges, I rarely take them on my own. Inevitably there are challenges for the people around me too. In building businesses I have noticed there are times when finances are stretched. Obviously, there is a knock-on effect to Caroline and the family. At times like these, there is a chance that any negative energy could intensify. The reality is that my challenges could start to have a negative impact on others.

It's Not Just *Your* Challenge

The level of positive and negative energy can appear to be heavily influenced by one question: is this "my challenge" or "our challenge"? Does your challenge impact on others directly? When I started to embark upon this rather ridiculous challenge, I became aware that it wasn't just my challenge. As much as I wanted this challenge to have minimal impact on those around me, the reality is that we humans are interconnected. Whatever we do, we're likely to impact other people somehow.

In 2006, Colin Beavan launched a year-long project to live "off-grid" in the middle of New York City. His aim was to make the minimum environmental impact possible: no carbon footprint. It won't surprise you to know that he is also known as "No Impact Man". The irony, of course, is that his no impact approach had a significant impact on the lifestyle of his wife and two-year-old daughter.

In fact, my decision had actually created several challenges for Caroline, which she hadn't chosen. I had imposed them upon her. There were some smaller, logistical challenges, such as looking after the girls when I went training. There were also some larger ones, such as making money available for equipment or expenses. Why on earth should we be spending money on a roof rack for kayaks when we have shoes to buy for the girls, and we need to replace a sofa that is well past its best? These are all very good questions!

We face very similar challenges in building a business. We often make decisions to invest my time, or our finances, in order to grow the business. We are used to making those decisions and comfortable with the prospect of making compromises in our lifestyle. There are a lot of people running their own businesses that will appreciate these challenges. However, there is a distinct difference between the way Caroline views the compromises that come with growing the business, compared to the compromises that come with this challenge. The simple fact is that we made the decision to grow the business. It was a joint decision. In fact, many of the decisions we make in the business are made jointly. Therefore, we both accept the compromises that come with them. By contrast, I chose this endurance challenge. To compound this of course, Caroline really can't see the point in it. If we're honest, she'd probably prefer that I'd never had the idea in the first place. She simply can't understand why I would go to all this trouble, and risk putting myself in danger. What is it all for?

The simple fact is that it will be harder to get a great deal of support if those closest to you don't genuinely support the idea. If they would rather you didn't do the challenge at all, you're likely to experience resistance from them. So how do you deal with this?

The Value of Negativity

The toughest questions are often the most valuable. Although they can feel the most uncomfortable, they are the very questions that we need to answer. The discomfort helps to highlight the areas that we need to give greatest attention to. When our weaknesses and vulnerabilities are highlighted, we know what we need to strengthen.

When our
weaknesses and
vulnerabilities
are highlighted,
we know what
we need to
strengthen.

Therefore, those people that appear to be the most negative can also be the ones that ask these vital questions. Of course, hearing it is not always pleasant. We tend to prefer the positive people, with their words of encouragement and praise. However, there is a great deal of potential value in the doubts, fears and criticism.

I have noticed over the years that world class performers deliberately seek out the negative voices. They seek out critics and sceptics because they often provide feedback that has the greatest value. It is their input that is most challenging. To world class performers, critical feedback is like oxygen. It stimulates improvements and helps them to get better. In fact, the very best in the world recruit people into their teams because they provide a critical or sceptical voice.

Double Olympic champion, Steve Williams, encountered similar conversations when he announced his intention to summit Mount Everest.

"When I said I was going to climb Everest and walk to the North Pole, people did say, 'Are you sure?' There is an inherent danger and I used their words as caution. It made me think about it a little harder. It focuses you on what you need to know and reinforces your attitude – the objective is not only to reach the summit, it's also to get home."

What impact does negative energy have on you? Does it tend to have a deflating effect, or do you see it as valuable input? Do you tend to curse it or welcome it?

The Importance of Balance

If you think about this concept broadly, you will start to see the teams around you. Families are an obvious example. Like many teams, there are some members that you recruit and some that you inherit. Managers, in business and sport, often start by inheriting their team. Over time they have the opportunity to shape the team by recruiting new members with specific skills, attitudes and aptitudes. Many leaders and managers are aware that good teams require a balance of personalities; some that are positive and energetic, and also some that are more considered and conservative. Astute leaders will often recognize when there is an imbalance. If the team is dominated by positive thinkers, they will deliberately recruit those who can ask some pointed questions and provide some challenge. Equally, if the team requires an injection of positive energy, a leader may seek a person that can provide a healthy dose of encouragement. In taking on your challenges, you may also need to shape your team, to ensure that it is well balanced.

Are you getting the value of both the positive and negative influences?

Your Authentic Response

Our opinions can sometimes become coloured by those around us. I often see it like the process of colouring hair. If you keep dying your hair and changing from one colour to the next, you could reach a point where you're not quite sure what your own authentic, natural colour is. Just as your natural hair colour is the foundation, so is your authentic response. Understand what you believe before you consider other people's perspectives.

What do you really think, feel and believe?

You have the choice to either change the way you think, or not.

invited to feel guilty for not spending time with my family. It is in these moments that I need to understand my authentic response. Am I being unreasonable? Should I change my decision or not? There are times when I have to admit that I've not been fair. There are times when I have pushed too far and overstepped the mark. However, there are times when I can honestly say I have acted reasonably, but others have not been happy with my decisions.

There are many occasions when I have asked myself the questions. Is this really dangerous, or is the feedback coming from someone who is simply expressing their own fear? Am I being too hasty, or is the feedback coming from someone that is just not ready for me to take this step? My authentic response is my foundation. I need to know my own position. What do I truly think and believe? I will only come to that position by asking the questions and reflecting on the answers. Sometimes the other person will be right. But sometimes I need to explain that I have listened, I have taken their views on board, thought about them, but decided to do what I believe is right instead.

Understanding my authentic response is not always easy. Sometimes I only realize my genuine position when I compromise it. I might agree to follow someone else's advice, thinking that they're probably right. I've noticed that whenever I do this, I get an uneasy sense that I've made the wrong decision. Normally, my mind starts to revisit it. My brain can't seem to settle. The thought nags at me, letting me know that I have probably taken a wrong turn. Have you ever noticed that when you make good decisions, your mind is happy to just let them go and move onto the next thing? On the other hand, if you make a decision that's not right for you, it keeps pestering you. I find that it's a useful way of helping me understand my authentic response.

Are you aware of your authentic response? What do you think, deep down inside? Isolate yourself from the myriad of opinions around you for a moment, and find your own position.

Take the Wheel

Importantly, we decide upon the influence that other people have on us. We have the power to sculpt and balance our team. We also have the ability to ask for input from others, to seek out those who can offer encouragement, positivity, energy, critical input or a sceptical voice. Crucially, we also have the power to choose whether we accept the information and emotion that other people offer. We don't have to feel guilty just because someone is angry with us. They may have a valid reason to be upset. We might even have to hold our hands up and take some responsibility, but it doesn't mean we should choose to feel guilt. We can take the wheel. We can take responsibility and take control for the way that we allow others to influence us.

Chapter Summary

★ Find the right people and the right team, not just your friends.

★ How much are your challenges impacting upon others?

★ Do you seek out critical and sceptical voices?

★ The toughest questions can be the most valuable.

★ What is your authentic response? What do you think?

Chapter 7

To Quit, or Not to Quit …?

"It does not matter how slowly you go, as long as you do not stop."

Confucius

I f you don't have any doubts, can you really claim that what you're attempting is tough enough to justify the word "challenge"? As polar explorer, Ben Saunders, once said to me, "If I know how we're going to do it, the challenge isn't hard enough." Surely doubts are just part of the territory. They form part of our mental "checks and balances" process. Our doubts make us stop and ask those important little questions. Sometimes, though, our doubts can start to become overwhelming and potentially disabling. They could start to erode our belief and disempower us. So, how do we navigate this mental territory and negotiate with our doubts? What happens if we seem to be going backwards?

Two Steps Forward, One Step Back

Have you noticed that progression is very rarely linear? If you've ever tried to lose weight, you'll probably have seen your scales taking on a

mind of their own. They just don't seem to understand that we have a specific goal in mind and that we need the needle to move in the right direction. We set ourselves a target: to lose two pounds per week for the next couple of months. We've done our bit. We ate less and did our exercise. We denied ourselves the cakes and yummy treats. Now it's the turn of the little needle on the scales.

Unfortunately, our physiology doesn't work in a regulated, linear fashion. We could do all the right things and only lose one pound this week. Equally, we may let our processes slip and get away with it occasionally. We forget, of course, that the little needle is not measuring our effort or how diligent we've been. It doesn't represent our hard work, or our desire to reach our goals. The little needle simply shows us our weight; that's it. The problem, for many people, is that they use the little number on the scales as a way of either congratulating themselves or berating themselves.

Measuring our progress makes sense. We need to know if we're moving forward and on the right track. However, if we start to judge ourselves as "a success" or "a failure" according to these results, we also open up the possibility that we'll become disheartened when the results don't show us what we expect. We may also start to doubt our ability to reach the goal. If we've been trying really hard and we can't see the results yet, we may start to question if we're ever going to get there.

What happens when we actually appear to be going backwards? What happens if the needle on the scale actually moves in the wrong direction? That's not in the script is it? My brother, Jon, found similar challenges when learning German. He described how he initially underestimated how difficult it would be.

He'd imagined going to the classes, absorbing it and then just expected it to flow out of his mouth. The reality was very different; he was failing at his homework and didn't feel as if he was picking it up at the speed he needed to. He'd get home from classes feeling completely drained, sit down with his homework and just couldn't connect to it. The whole experience left him feeling utterly demotivated.

Andy Reid describes how deflating it was when he suffered setbacks.

"I had been working really hard in the gym to build myself up to get my prosthetic legs, and I'd arranged to go to Headley Court to get them fitted. When I got there I explained to the nurse that my stump felt a bit sore. She took a look and said to me, 'Sorry Andy, you're going to have to go back to Selly Oak, you've got an infection in it.' I was told I needed to spend the next six weeks back in the wheelchair. Well, she may as well have kicked me in the balls. All that work in the gym to get me back on my feet and it was all for nothing. I was completely gutted. As we drove back to Selly Oak, I thought, 'Sod this, maybe I should just stick to my wheelchair and give up on walking.'"

In reality, there are common features to progression curves. When we start out, we tend to make quite large strides. We put in relatively little effort and get pretty good returns. After a while, the returns get smaller and the effort required gets bigger. It is common for us to encounter plateaus, where we get very little visible progression even though we're putting in the effort. As we develop more expertise, we need to invest huge amounts of time, energy and application just to achieve marginal gains. Interestingly, we often get a very different perspective of our progress when we take a macro view, as opposed to a micro view. If we plotted our body weight every hour, we'd notice quite a lot of fluctuation. We might even become confused as to why it had gone up or down, based on our activities during the course of that hour. If, however, we weighed ourselves every six months, we'd take out all of those little fluctuations and simply see our net progress over the longer term. Most progression curves are uneven. There are rises and falls in performance. However, most of them show a general movement in the right direction when you take a step back and look at the longer-term picture.

The Challenges Change, They Don't Disappear

I have been working with an executive coaching client for a few years now. He's a managing director who runs a very successful recruitment business. Over the years he has had his fair share of challenges. All of them seem tough as he's going through them. It would be easy for him to conclude that he's not moving forward, because the challenges don't seem to be any easier. However, if we take a step back, we can see the progress he has made. There are situations that presented significant challenges a few years ago, which he doesn't perceive as challenging now. The business is overcoming situations that would have been catastrophic in the past. Whilst these situations are very demanding, the business is now capable of riding out the storm. Rather than spending time firefighting, he is now able to become more strategic and focus on growing his business. He has some cash reserves now, so he's not managing the cash flow in a "hand to mouth" fashion. Interestingly, he can now go on holiday and doesn't feel the need to check in with his team every day to make sure they're okay. He knows that they can do a good job. That's progress!

Progress is almost a given when we consistently do the right things.

Sometimes we are making progress, but we're just not able to see it. Maybe we are looking at the wrong things. Perhaps we just need to sharpen our focus. If an athlete only measures progress in whole seconds, they may get half a second quicker but conclude that they're not improving. Olympic swimmer, Chris Cook, once said to me:

"It comes from working every day and putting in the tiny little building blocks. And I'm going to say this now; it feels like you're getting nowhere … But eventually, all those little building blocks add up and they get their opportunity to shine."

There is often a delay, a lag phase, between making the progress and seeing the progress. Sometimes we have to trust our processes; know that we're doing the right thing. If we keep investing, eventually we will see the return. Sometimes we do have to change the plan slightly and adapt. However, progress is almost a given when we consistently do the right things.

My brother, Jon, found a similar phenomenon when learning to speak German:

"I didn't understand the mountains I needed to climb. I just couldn't work out why I couldn't do this. I should be able to do this. I am not stupid, I'm a pretty smart guy. It is incredibly frustrating. The fact is, some of the things have just taken a long time to click. It could be that I learn something on one course, don't get it by the second course, but it clicks during the third course. I'm not a natural at learning languages."

No doubt there are things that you once found demanding, which you now take in your stride. Given a few moments' reflection, it's possible to see the progress we have made.

Is It a Setback or an Opportunity?

I don't think that I have ever met an elite athlete who hasn't been injured. In many cases, the best in the world have been through the most serious injuries. In sport, injury and illness are part of the landscape. It is expected. Rather than asking if they will get injured, it is probably more sensible to ask when. Obviously, all good athletes try to prevent, or minimize, the risk but realistically they know it is likely to happen at some point. However, the way that athletes respond to injury varies noticeably from one to the next.

Some athletes will consider that they're just "unlucky", and will tend to mope about feeling sorry for themselves until they're fit enough to train again. Others will become quite angry and frustrated because they feel like they're losing ground on their competitors. This often leads them to becoming impatient. These

It was my body's way of flagging an issue that needed my attention. Simply trying to silence that message won't achieve anything. I needed to change my running action. I needed to stop rolling my foot out. So, I delved back into my memory banks, to the days when I used to study anatomy and biomechanics as a sport science student.

I started to realize that some of my muscles weren't doing their jobs properly and so I needed to strengthen them. There were some that had probably become too loose and needed tightening. So, I started doing some exercises to redress the imbalances. I also figured out that my driving position in the car was probably not helping. It was a comfortable, but lazy, way of sitting that was contributing to the problem. I needed to change my position and actually sit properly. It meant that driving became quite uncomfortable for a while as my body adjusted. I was tempted to just relax back into the old position, but of course that was only going to exacerbate the problem, not solve it. When I ran, I began to concentrate on every stride, to make sure that my foot was in the right position and that I could feel my weight being transferred properly. It was effortful. At the time I half wished that I could have just relaxed, switched off and plodded along instead of concentrating. However, it wasn't very long before I saw some changes.

What I noticed was very interesting. The blister started to move. Over the course of a week or so, it crept from the outside of my foot, under the arch, to the inside of my foot at the base of my big toe. It didn't stop there for long before it started moving back underneath the arch in the centre of my foot and then … it disappeared.

When we're presented with these little "problems" it is often tempting to simply wish them away. If we get a headache, we ultra-marathons with a torn Achilles tendon and suspected fractured shin. US Navy SEAL, Gary Rossi, described how his friend Michael E. Thornton ran into a battle to rescue his lieutenant. Michael carried his wounded teammate back to the shore and then swam two hours to a rendezvous boat, towing his unconscious comrade. If that's not heroic enough, did I mention that Michael was also shot twice; in the thigh and the shoulder? Robyn Benincasa told me how she competed in adventure races through ill health and injury.

"We had to push the limits. Everyone had some kind of pulmonary oedema. I had a fever of 104 degrees and bronchitis. Normally I'd have been in hospital; I certainly wouldn't have been at work."

It is easy to see how our view of "toughness" can be dominated by certain characteristics. With my sport psychology consultant's hat on, I believe that there are three elements to mental toughness:

1 **Tenacity** – the ability to push as hard as you can and keep pushing, even when you just want to stop.

2 **Resilience** – the ability to bounce back, to overcome adversity and perform at your best when things go against you.

3 **Composure** – the ability to make great decisions, and execute with high quality, whatever is going on. It is this element of toughness that actually requires us to often stop, take a moment and think.

The bulldozer approach often causes us to lose our composure. If we assume that toughness is simply the ability to endure the discomfort and keep fighting, we may actually end up making some pretty poor decisions.

My First Ultra

Captain's Log, Star Date: Twenty Seven Zero Five (or something)

I woke up this morning and decided that I wanted to try running an ultra-marathon (that's 50 kilometres or 31 miles). It's a bank holiday, I've got the day off, nothing else planned, so why not?

Recently I have been running between five and ten miles, so this is a massive step up. I am planning to break it up slightly, by running it in stages with regular stops for drinks, food and a stretch. I have worked out a circuit of 8.64 miles which I'll run four times between now and the end of the day. I'll let you know how I'm doing at the end of each circuit. Wish me luck.

8.64 miles down, lots to go
My knees are feeling pretty wobbly, my calves have tightened up and my right foot is not happy. I am going to have to take it easy and look after them, particularly on the downhill sections.

On the up side, it is a gorgeous day. The sun is out but it is a bit chilly, which could well help later on. The late spring colours are amazing. There are so many different shades of green in the trees, as well as the purples, the last of the blossom, the bluebells and the bright yellow rape seed crops that are in flower. The hedgerows are also in bloom now and the smells are fantastic. Occasionally there is a lovely aroma of cut grass or wood smoke and I've seen loads of different birds nipping in and out of the hedges.

At this point I am thinking that running three more circuits will be tough, but it is possible.

Half-way
As I set off for the second circuit I felt a shooting pain through my left leg. It seemed to disappear after about half a mile, so I am assuming it was just my body settling into the run.

Although I am enjoying my surroundings and the wildlife, I have noticed that I am definitely concentrating more on nursing my right knee, especially on the gentle downhill sections.

Second half
I made a rather unusual decision: to roll the last two circuits into one. If I am honest, it is because I wanted to get finished and sit on my backside this evening

rather than going out running again. That may not have been the wisest decision I have ever made. Today I lacked composure and patience. If I was one of the mountaineers in the story (back in Chapter 2), I would have climbed the mountain in poor conditions and probably died in the process.

It is amazing how influential fatigue can be. I noticed that my decision making and mood were both significantly affected by tiredness. Rather than sticking to the game plan and pacing myself, I decided to try to push on and get finished. On reflection, that's the polar opposite of what I actually needed. I am tired; therefore I need more rest, more stretching, more regular food and drink stops.

As a result I found the second half really tough. My legs were sore; they felt really heavy and were constantly aching. I had to concentrate hard, making sure that I placed my feet very deliberately and safely, so that I didn't blow my knee out. I reached a point, on the way home, where I had to stop and walk. After a while I thought I'd try to break into a jog again. It was a very tired, almost pathetic, attempt and I just couldn't keep it going. I crawled home for the last couple of miles.

Interestingly, I hardly noticed the glorious countryside or the wildlife. I saw glimpses, for a few seconds at a time, but couldn't seem to dwell on it. I was literally running the same route as I did this morning; the same colours,

The Quiet Voice

I don't know about your head, but mine can be a pretty noisy place. As well as the background noise, the chit chat and general wittering, there are also the debates and tussles.

Should I or shouldn't I?

Is that really a good idea or not?

Am I about to regret this, or not? Where's the line between courage and stupidity?

I am a great believer that we need to dare.

I know that many exceptional people, and world class performers, live by this philosophy. They do dare to dream, to push themselves, to take the risks. However, I have also heard highly successful business leaders, entrepreneurs and investors explaining that they actually take very few risks, because their decisions are calculated. In a recent Dinner with Be World Class event, Olympic gold medal winning coach, Chris Bartle, explained that risks can be mitigated by great preparation.

My conscious brain, that bit that conducts these conversations, can tie itself up in knots sometimes. It has the ability to form two very convincing, but completely opposing, arguments at the same time. How can one brain produce a list of pros and cons that have seemingly equal strength? How is it possible for one mind to create a complete stalemate with itself? That's insane!

"To dare
is to lose
one's footing
momentarily.
Not to dare is to
lose oneself."

Søren Kierkegaard, existential philosopher

Fortunately, beyond the noise and confusion there is another place. It lies beyond thought. This place, deep within our mind, doesn't seem to have a conversation. It almost seems as if language and words just don't apply here.

In this place, feelings dominate. It is often called our intuition. When our conscious brain is locked in stalemate, it is our intuition that holds the solution. In amongst all the noise and argument, there is a very quiet voice that seems to whisper the answer.

Sometimes I recognize it, and follow the advice of my quiet voice. Sometimes my intuitive voice will tell me it's okay to press on, and that I can do it. Sometimes it will advise me to stop completely. Sometimes it tells me to wait.

Occasionally I think I know better, and disregard my intuition. Personally, I tend to find that disregarding it is the foolish route. I'll normally end up concluding that I should have followed the sage advice of my quiet voice after all. Often I'll have caused myself more hardship than necessary in the process.

Normally when I ignore my intuition, I'll find that the loud voices keep on debating, and I often try desperately to justify my decision. When I follow my intuition, the conversation dies down. In those really tough moments, maybe it's wise to stop, take a moment and listen to that quiet voice before deciding whether to charge headlong into the battle.

In those
really tough
moments, maybe it's wise
to stop, take a moment and
listen to that quiet voice before
deciding whether to charge
headlong into the battle.

Do you notice your quiet voice? When do you hear it ... and when do you listen to it?

What happens if you're faced with a tough decision? Is it a case of understanding what's easy and what's right? Or is the decision tough because we're missing a vital piece of the jigsaw?

If I am finding a decision difficult, it's often because I don't have all the information. Rather than making the decision, maybe we just need to find the information that's missing. Once we've got all the information we need, the decision seems easier.

What does our mind do when we hit the real roadblocks?

Setbacks

I've spoken to many people about taking on challenges. Some of those people have taken on some incredible and extreme challenges, including some of the folks that have contributed to this book. Whether the challenge is extreme, or much more modest, in almost every case there have been setbacks. In fact, it is rare to find any "setback-free" examples. I would go as far as to say that they should be expected; they're part of the landscape. Perhaps we shouldn't ask whether we'll experience setbacks, but when. Equally, if we know that they are inevitable, we ought to ask how we'll respond to them when they do come along.

Some of the time, these setbacks can be relatively minor. They are the situations that might slow you down temporarily, or cause you to change course for a while. Others are potential showstoppers. These events have the potential to cause a fatal blow and derail a challenge completely. Interestingly, an event that might become a "showstopper" for some people would be viewed as a minor inconvenience by others.

To Quit, or Not to Quit? That Is the Question

Robyn Benincasa knows that there are some times when you have to stop, and others when you could stop.

"Trench foot was a deal breaker, I just couldn't go on. However, short of incapacitation or catastrophic gear failure, as long as you can keep moving forward there is always a way.

When it's really tough and I don't know if I can keep going, I stop and think. I could take the radio out and quit now. And then what? I fast forward my mind into next week, sitting comfortably with a glass of wine, knowing that I quit. And then I think, 'Oh, hell no! That's not my story.' I still have a chance to avoid that scenario. I have the chance not to quit.

Your mind always quits before your body. It comes down to the Henry Ford saying, 'Whether you think you can, or you think you can't, either way you'll be right.'

To me, quitting is scarier than pain or suffering. If I quit at this, what else am I going to quit? What am I going to be fearful of? What happens when the next challenge in life comes my way? By not quitting, I know that whatever does come my way, I'll give it my very best shot. That way, you don't have to know what's coming or how to handle it. In adventure racing, we have no idea what we're going to encounter, but we do know that we can figure it out together. We can't study every inch of the problem in advance. I don't have to know everything if I know that I am equipped to deal with whatever comes."

It is this mentality that enables Robyn to keep going when others stop. So what is it that dictates whether a setback is potentially terminal, or just a bump in the road?

Personally, I believe that we choose the extent to which an event or situation will affect us. To Robyn Benincasa, mere injuries aren't enough to prevent her from achieving her goals. She might argue that "it's just a body". Her challenge doesn't stop just because she happens to lose the use of a leg, or because she has a fever. Other people might argue that those are perfectly good reasons to stop. The question is one of importance. What's more important, my hip or completing the challenge? Some people might say it's their hip. I would argue that there is no right or wrong answer. However, it is vital that we understand how far we are willing to go. What is most important? What are you willing to accept? What are you not willing to lose?

What Happens if a Bombshell Drops?

When you think of the word "bombshell", you imagine an experience similar to Andy Reid's, where something that lands unexpectedly explodes, and changes your world in a split second. Our "bombshell" crept up on us over many months.

Around six months into the training my wife, Caroline, began to notice some unusual sensations and numbness in her hands and feet. It seemed pretty innocuous at first. She would wake up occasionally and wonder whether she'd been sleeping on her arm. On other days she would experience numbness or tingling feelings in her feet. As the weeks went on Caroline found other unusual symptoms. She would wake up exhausted and found it difficult to maintain her energy levels through the day.

One Sunday morning I had planned to go for a training session on the bike. We'd planned a route that would take us approximately 60 miles into the North Yorkshire Moors. It was a good three- to four-hour ride. I was dressed up in my cycling gear and dayglo jacket, looking particularly ridiculous. Not only did I have the Lycra bottoms, I also had Caroline's pink fluffy socks and just about every other piece of warm clothing I could muster. I was just about to set off when Caroline came down the stairs. She looked terrible (sorry love, it's true). Rather than laughing at the way I was dressed and wishing me well on the ride, she crashed out on the sofa exhausted. She could hardly raise herself to drink a cup of tea, never mind look after herself and the girls. Needless to say, I cancelled the ride. Clearly Caroline was in no position to be left on her own for several hours to look after two energetic girls.

As Caroline's symptoms became more pronounced, we began the long process of medical investigations, tests, results and consultations. In early January, we had the first hint of a diagnosis. However, it came with a caveat. Caroline wasn't just suffering with one condition; she

He said, "It's unlikely that you'll stop because you can't go on. It's more likely that you'll stop because you're bored." Bizarre as it sounds, he was absolutely right. When we think about the real reasons we quit, often it isn't because we can't go on. There are very few things that actually stop us. On the vast majority of occasions we stop because we don't want to continue.

Do you remember Andy Reid describing the setback he experienced when his wound became infected? After working so hard, and building himself up to start learning to walk with prosthetic legs, he was set back six weeks by the infection. Initially, Andy felt like giving up the idea of walking and resigning himself to life in a wheelchair. However, Andy's desire to walk was incredibly powerful. There were strong reasons why he couldn't just give up. He's a proud man who values independence and his ability to look after his loved ones.

"A few days later I watched Claire [Andy's wife] struggling to lift my wheelchair. I just couldn't watch it, I felt terrible because she was ill as well. It gave me a real push to get back on my feet again. I couldn't watch her struggling, I just needed to do it, to get back on my feet again."

We do not give up because we fail ... we fail because we give up.

We always have choices when faced with a situation or circumstance. If something stops us in our tracks, we can decide whether to let it stop us permanently or just temporarily. Is this "The End" or just a disruption?

We do not give up because we fail …

we fail because we give up.

Change Course

What if we viewed challenges, or the process of taking on challenges, in the same way? What if we viewed plans in the same way? If we took Darwin's perspective, it is not the strongest that survive (or the most intelligent) but those that are most adaptable to change, or most willing to change.

> "It is not the strongest or the most intelligent who will survive but those who can best manage change."
>
> *Charles Darwin (1859)*

This book talks largely about the challenges we choose in life. However, as Andy Reid will testify, some of our challenges choose us. Although he chose to join the Army, and knew of the potential dangers, he didn't choose to lose both his legs and one of his arms. However, Andy quickly accepted the challenge that he was presented with and applied his mind to tackling it. Andy's "Plan A" for his life changed in a split second. The same process applies when we need to make significant changes. How quickly can we accept that our original plan needs to change? Is it plan A or bust? Are we willing to re-think the whole thing? Would we be willing to start again?

At some point, you might find yourself considering exactly this question with your own challenge. But the question should not be "Should I continue?" but "How do I continue?"

If You Want Great Answers, Ask Great Questions

The questions that we ask normally dictate the answers that we get. If we ask, "How could I?" our brain will apply itself to answering the question. It will start to find possible answers, playing around with ideas and forming potential solutions. If we ask, "Why didn't I?" our brain will find different answers.

"Lots of guys that lost limbs in Afghanistan are still blaming what happened. I decided to join the Army; no one made me. There's no point in blaming the terrorist for planting the device either. There is no point in dwelling. Blame doesn't move you forwards. I need to just focus on what I need to do."

Andy Reid, triple amputee soldier, author, speaker, charity fundraiser and inspiration to many

Whilst some people look for excuses, others look for lessons. What can I do differently next time? How can I improve? What can I learn from this which will make me stronger? Can this experience help me refine my game plan, or help me identify skills that I need to work on?

I recently delivered a keynote presentation to a conference full of expert practitioners in Dubai. They understand that the very best practitioners are often the most experienced. During the presentation I explained that experience is not a function of time, but of learning. Often we think that the most experienced people are those that have been around longest. However, that's not always true. The most experienced people tend to be those who have learned the most. In order to learn from our experiences, we need to be able to take responsibility.

Re-Group

There seems to be a natural cycle in all challenges where we need to stop, take stock and re-group before we carry on. If we make sure we learn the lessons, we're likely to adjust our plan before we set off again. The very best teams and individuals I've worked with conduct very thorough reviews and then make sure that the review informs their future plans.

It is at times like these when your team comes into its own. Both the supportive and critical voices have their value. On occasions we may need to seek those voices of encouragement. At other times we may need to tap into those people that tell us things we don't like, but do need to hear. I've just been reminded how it feels to receive critical feedback. It tends to leave me feeling like

"I have the courage, I believe, to doubt everything;... but I have not the courage to know anything."

Søren Kierkegaard

Observe Your Thoughts

If we accept that doubts are normal, and even world champions have them, it becomes easier to engage with them. At the point that I stop judging doubts as "threatening", or "wrong" or as "a sign of weakness", I can use them to help me. Once I engage with my doubts, I can start asking myself the questions openly and start searching for the answers.

"Okay, so what if it doesn't work? What would I do? What are my options? What are my choices?"

As we can see from those who have successfully taken on challenges, it is not the presence of doubt, but our response to it, that counts. My brother, Jon, suffered a real setback when he started his business in Germany. Jon's background is broadcasting, particularly in television and specifically in sport. He had spent a year or so making connections and building relationships with German sports broadcasters. He'd been out to meet them, spent a week or so working with them, and felt that he'd have a firm foundation when he made the move to Cologne. However, things didn't go as planned. He did get an audition as a commentator, which seemed like an amazing opportunity. However, instead of feedback and a follow-up conversation, he encountered radio silence. It is one of many cultural differences that he experienced. Rather than being open to good ideas that might have mutual benefit, Jon found that the German businesses tended to work purely from their own pre-set agenda. He began to learn that he'd have to wait until they were ready.

"It's frustrating when you need it to work, and you can see an obvious opportunity that would benefit both of you. My confidence in moving out to Germany was based on the theory that they would recognize the opportunities that I could see. It dawned on me very quickly that they didn't see them. Bang goes the game plan! That was the whole basis of my plan. I have to say that I was rudderless for a while. I asked myself, 'How do I get past this?'"

It's possible that many people would start to panic at that point and question their decision to quit their job and move abroad. However, there are normally lessons that accompany our experience. If we look for them, there is a good chance we'll benefit from them. Jon explained how he adjusted his approach, based on what he'd learned.

"The solution was to find the people who know that they need the solution, not those who don't know they need it. We now have some projects with Gazprom, BVB (Borussia Dortmund Football Club) and the Bundesliga because there is a really good fit between what they know they need and what we do."

Challenge Your Doubts

There's a temptation to take self-doubt, or the doubts of others, and turn them into self-criticism. Our own mind often makes feedback feel personal. Of course, we interpret the feedback that comes in, apply meanings to it and ultimately decide whether to make it personal or not. We also decide whether we're going to magnify doubts, or to take them out of context.

I heard a mum, who was having a self-critical moment, say that she was letting her family down and not feeding them properly because she "always cooked them pasta". She was beating herself up with this statement, and criticizing herself for not giving them a balanced, varied and healthy diet.

I asked her when she cooked pasta for them last. She said that she couldn't remember exactly, but that it was probably a week or ten days ago. Then I asked, on average, how many times a week she would normally cook pasta. When she thought about it, the answer was, "I suppose I cook it once every week or two."

Our brains have a habit of over-generalizing, creating inaccurate, misleading and false statements that we then use to form the basis of our doubts and self-criticism. Phrases like, "I never" or "I always" are often not true. Often we skew our own perception by taking a small piece of reality and blowing it up in our minds. Athletes often fall into this trap when they evaluate their performances. If an athlete loses, they tend to focus on the mistakes that they made and go over them in their mind. When I ask them how they performed, they'll often tell me that they were awful and made tons of stupid errors. In contrast, those who win often tell me that they performed quite well. They'll probably remember more of the positive points and forget some of the errors. In reality, there is often very little difference between the winning performances and the losses. The athlete's mind, however, exacerbates the differences and creates a gulf between them.

Robyn Benincasa:

"Build up your base of
experience and confidence.
It's not zero to ironman!

You have to put in the time, build the
base and do the struggle. You have to
invest. Put your time in, consistently.

There is no magic formula;
it's discipline, time and
understanding yourself."

Jon, my brother:

"Be prepared that you
will underestimate the
scale of the challenge.

Minimize the risks by preparing well
and over-catering for the demands.

Know that you will need to
reassess and change tack.

Find the right people, with
shared passions and ideals.

Ask yourself, 'Are you willing to
take the emotional hits?'"

Andy Reid:

"If the gap between you and your goal seems too big, too daunting, you might get overwhelmed. Break it down; take it step by step.

You could easily talk yourself out of it by saying "I'm not good enough to do that." Start small and give yourself a chance.

When you decide upon something and commit to it, you'll do it."

Wise words, I'm sure you'll agree.

My Journey

At this point in my own journey, I have noticed myself reflecting on the way I have taken on my challenge and the lessons that I can learn. My view of "toughness" has changed. I learned that courage is not the absence of fear, but the realization that there is something more important than it. Equally, toughness is not the absence of doubt or the ability to ignore pain. Maybe even a wimp like me can do this? In order to take on my challenges and be successful, I do not need to become someone else. I don't need to be a superhero, or the ruthlessly single-minded person who will win at all costs. I have also realized that I can make it by consistently taking tiny steps forward. I don't need all the answers right now, or all of the skills, or the ability. I can develop and learn what I need over time. When I give myself permission to try something new and fail at it, I also allow myself to learn.

Your Journey

I know it sounds like a cliché, which you'll have heard thousands of times before, but the only thing that will ever hold me back is me. The same is true for you. I can see many more of the forks in the road now. There are so many occasions in life when we're presented with choices and decisions. Do we squash our ideas because they seem ridiculous and outlandish? Would the people around us laugh and tell us we were stupid; that we ought to "get real" rather than having our head stuck in the clouds? When we hit the challenges, and have the doubts, do we conclude that we were never cut out for this in the first place and throw in the towel?

We are presented with these questions, choices and decisions on a moment-by-moment basis. Arguably, our whole life is the culmination of the choices we make. In these moments we have chosen who we are and written the story of our lives. The next page is blank. What do you want to write on it? What do you want the next part of the story to tell?

Can we start to master our own mental territory and take control of the conversation that goes on between our ears? If we did, imagine how different our decisions might be. What might you do that you've never done before? Which challenges might you take on? What would happen if you took a few moments and asked yourself one innocent question …

Could I Do That?

Bibliography and References

Ankersen, R. (2011) *The Gold Mine Effect: Unlocking the Essence of World Class Performance.* London: Rasmus Ankersen.

Be World Class Conference (2011) Kenny Atkinson . . . on Standards, 6th October 2011. Online. Available at: http://www. beworldclass.tv (accessed 31st January 2012).

Be World Class Conference (2012) Kenny Atkinson . . . on the Journey, 25th October 2012. Online. Available at: http://www. be-world-class.com (accessed 20th August 2013).

Be World Class Conference (2011) Chris Cook . . . on Talent, 6th October 2011. Online. Available at: http://www.beworldclass.tv (accessed 31st January 2012).

Be World Class Conference (2011) Bruce Duncan . . . on Mental Toughness, 6th October 2011. Online. Available at: http://www. beworldclass.tv (accessed 31st January 2012).

Be World Class Conference (2011) James Hoffmann . . . on The Finest Details, 6th October 2011. Online. Available at: http:// www.beworldclass.tv (accessed 31st January 2012).

Be World Class Conference (2011) Keir Worth . . . on Staying Ahead, 6th October 2011. Online. Available at: http://www. beworldclass.tv (accessed 31st January 2012).

Be World Class Conference (2012) Simon Hartley . . . on Being World Class, 25th October 2012. Online. Available at: http:// www.be-world-class.com (accessed 20th August 2013).

Be World Class Conference (2012) Simon Hartley . . . on Becoming World Class, 25th October 2012. Online. Available at: http://www.be-world-class.com (accessed 20th August 2013).

Be World Class Conference (2012) James Hoffmann . . . on Compromise, 25th October 2012. Online. Available at: http://www.be-world-class.com (accessed 20th August 2013).

Be World Class Conference (2012) Andy McMenemy . . . on Mental Toughness, 25th October 2012. Online. Available at: http://www.be-world-class.com (accessed 20th August 2013).

Be World Class Conference (2012) Andy McMenemy . . . on The Impossible, 25th October 2012. Online. Available at: http://www.be-world-class.com (accessed 20th August 2013).

Be World Class Conference (2012) Claire O'Hara . . . on Attention to Detail, 25th October 2012. Online. Available at: http://www.be-world-class.com (accessed 20th August 2013).

Blaine, D. (2010) How I held my breath for 17 minutes, TED Talks. Online. Available at: http://www.ted.com/talks/david_blaine_how_i_held_my_breath_for_17_min.html. (accessed 1st October 2013).

Brownlee, A. and Brownlee, J. (2013) *Swim, Bike, Run: Our Triathlon Story.* London: Penguin Viking.

Burlingham, B. (2007) *Small Giants: Companies that Choose to Be Great Instead of Big.* London: Penguin.

Cartmer-Edwards, K. (2013) *Bigger, Better, Bolder, Faster*. St Albans, UK: Anoma Press.

Confucius (1979) *The Analects*. London: Penguin Books.

Covey, S.R. (2004) *The 7 Habits of Highly Effective People*. New York: Simon & Schuster.

Darwin, C. (1859) *On The Origin of Species by Means of Natural Selection or The Preservation Of Favoured Races in the Struggle for Life*. London: John Murray.

Dinner with Be World Class (2013a) On . . . World Class Leadership with Simon Hartley and Floyd Woodrow, 14th March 2013. Online. Available at: http://www.be-world-class.com (accessed 20th August 2013).

Dinner with Be World Class (2013b) On . . . World Class Preparation with Simon Hartley and Chris Bartle, 20th June 2013. Online. Available at: http://www.be-world-class.com (accessed 20th August 2013).

Eliot, T.S. (1931) Preface to *Transit of Venus* (Poems by Harry Crosby). London: Black Sun Press.

Frankl, V. E. (2004) *Man's Search for Meaning*. London: Rider.

Gladwell, M. (2008) *Outliers: The Story of Success*. London: Little, Brown & Co.

Guinness World Records (2012) Guinness World Records Totally Bonkers Sporting Champions. Online. Available at: http://www.guinnessworldrecords.com/news/2012/7/guinness-world-records-honours-the-alternative-sporting-champions-in-new-ebook-43310

Guinness World Records (2013) Summer of Champions. Online. Available at: http://www.guinnessworldrecords.com/summer-of-champions/records-broken-so-far

Hartley, S.R. (2011) *Peak Performance Every Time*. London: Routledge.

Hartley, S.R. (2012) *How To Shine: Insights into unlocking potential from proven winners*. Chichester, UK: Capstone.

Hartley, S.R. (2013) *Two Lengths of the Pool: Sometimes the simplest ideas have the greatest impact*. Arkendale, UK: Be World Class.

Hill, N. (1975) *Think and Grow Rich*. Robbinsdale, MI: Fawcett Books.

Lowenstein, G. (1994) The Psychology of Curiosity: A Review and Reinterpretation. *Psychological Bulletin*, **116**(1), 75–88.

Pausch, R. and Zaslow, J. (2008) *The Last Lecture*. London: Hodder & Stoughton.

Pugh, L. (2009) How I Swam the North Pole, TED Talks. Online. Available at: http://www.ted.com/talks/lewis_pugh_swims_the_north_pole.html (accessed 1st October 2013).

Reid, A. (2013) *Standing Tall: The Inspirational Story of a True British Hero*. London: John Blake Publishing.

Sinek, S. (2010) Are You Willing To Strike Out? Refocus, 30th March 2010. Online. Available at: http://sinekpartners.typepad.com/refocus/2010/03/are-you-willing-to-strike-out.html.

Woodrow, F. and Acland, S. (2012) *Elite! The Secret to Exceptional Leadership and Performance*. London: Elliot & Thompson.

Young, S. (2012) 'Can You Get an MIT Education for $2000?' TED Talks. 19 June 2012. Online. Available at: http://www.youtube.com/watch?v=piSLobJfZ3c.

Image List

P14 Vector abstract background of blue star burst – Dmitry Merkushin/iStock/ Getty Images

P15 Spark idea – Topp_Yimgrimm/iStock/Getty Images

P17 Comics faces – Seamartini/iStock/Getty Images

P17 Less light icon – Tkacchuk/iStock/Getty Images

P22 Idea tree – Designaart/iStock/Getty Images

P24 Heart Beats, Isolated On White Background – Iadams/Shutterstock.com

P40 Businessman lose idea – ratch0013/iStock/Getty Images

P49 Concrete block pavement – Pialhovik/iStock/Getty Images

P50 Jigsaw puzzle – Maxym Boner/iStock/Getty Images

P53 Dance footstep background – Transfuchsian/iStock/Getty Images

P55 Rugby players collection – Violeta Stosic/Hemera/Getty Images

P57 Businessman superhero concept – Christos Georghiou/iStock/Getty Images

P62 Businessman competition – Suryazaidan/iStock/Getty Images

P69 Vector symbols of people – Dmitry Merkushin/iStock/Getty Images

P71 Cartoon goalposts with a net – Adrian Niederhäuser/iStock/Getty Images

P74 Best of 2013 – Place4design/iStock/Getty Images

P81 Swirl background – Ankur Patil/iStock/Getty Images

P82-83 Yellow wooden pencil on the blank notepad – Yganko/iStock/Getty Images

P86 Baby infographic – Losw/iStock/Getty Images

P91 Comic superhero character – Benoit Chartron/iStock/Getty Images

P92 Lightbulb brain idea for ideas or inspiration – Ratch0013/iStock/Getty Images

P93 Brick wall – Alexander Bryljaev/iStock/Getty Images

P95 Empty sign – Ilona Lapshina/iStock/Getty Images

P104 Smiley icons – Sergey Lagutin/iStock/Getty Images

P113 Weakest link – Lurii Druzhynets/iStock/Getty Images

P118 Thoughts and options head with arrows – ARTQU/iStock/Getty Images

P126 Catch new idea – Designaart/iStock/Getty Images

P143 Yoga and pilates background – Yo-ichi/iStock/Getty Images

P157, 168, 171-174 Elements speech bubbles make in man think concept – Ponsuwan/iStock/Getty Images

Original illustrations supplied by Jonathan Marsh (www.jon-marsh.com): pages 44, 78, 87, 89, 112, 130, 155, 161, 163

All other images created by Andy Prior

About Simon Hartley

Reproduced with permission of Lee Mitchell

Simon Hartley is a globally respected sport psychology consultant and performance coach. He helps athletes and business people to get their mental game right. For almost 20 years, Simon has worked with gold medallists, world record holders, top five world-ranked professional athletes and championship winning teams. He has worked at the highest level of sport, including spells in Premiership football, Premiership rugby union, First Class County Cricket, Super League, golf, tennis, motor sport and with Team GB Olympians.

Since 2005, Simon has also applied the principles of sport psychology to business, education, healthcare and the charity sector. This has included projects with some of the world's leading corporations and foremost executives. He is also an international professional speaker, delivering keynotes across the world.

Simon's first book, *Peak Performance Every Time*, was published in 2011, followed in 2012 by *How To Shine*, and in 2013 by *Two Lengths of the Pool*. Simon has also delivered an array of Be World Class events and conferences.

For more information on Simon, please visit

www.be-world-class.com

SMARTER goals give us ways
to achieve our dreams.

DUMBER goals give us
dreams worth achieving.